THE DEMAGOGUES

THE DEMAGOGUES

FRED J. COOK

THE MACMILLAN COMPANY, NEW YORK, NEW YORK
COLLIER-MACMILLAN LIMITED, LONDON

CONTENTS

1
WHAT IS A DEMAGOGUE?

There are times when a kind of madness seems to sweep a nation. And these are the times of the demagogue.

The dictionary defines a demagogue as the leader of a popular faction or mob; an unprincipled orator or an agitator. Hitler was such a demagogue. But even Hitler could never have become the menace that he was had there not been a fever in the German people.

This fever, this mad unreason that seems at times to unhinge an entire nation, has one prime ingredient—fear. And fear has many roots. It may spring from racial or religious prejudice; it may be caused by a depression, by times so hard it seems as if the entire economic system is about to collapse; it may result from the dread of a foreign menace or of a hostile political system like communism. But, whatever its cause, one thing is certain—the fear is always there.

The demagogue seizes upon the fear of his time. He plays upon it to build up his own power. He appeals to the emotions of the fearful rather than to their reason; he whips up their passions. He picks out some handy scape-goat—some few individuals or some class in the nation whom he blames for all the evils the people see and fear. He calls for violent action to imprison or banish or even kill these enemies of the people. In the storm he raises, the most sacred principles of the nation are tossed overboard. Law, order, justice, the protection of the innocent—these are the first ideals to fall when the voice of the demagogue sweeps the land.

We Americans like to think that we are a different kind of people; that no demagogue can work his will on us. But we are wrong. Our history shows that we, too, have had our demagogues; that this usually stable democracy of ours has been twisted and torn by the rantings of passion peddlers—and by the violence that has always followed upon their words.

True, we have always recovered our senses before we have gone so far as to confer all power and glory upon a Hitler. But there have been times when we stepped dangerously close to the brink. And on those occasions the helpless and the innocent have suffered.

Our experience with mass insanity goes back to 1692 when the people of Salem Village, now Danvers, Massachusetts, became possessed by the idea that witches in their midst were causing all kinds of misfortunes and even death. Twenty persons, including old women and one minister, were executed before that fever of fear and suspicion ran its course.

Salem put the expression witch hunt into our language, but it was only the first of many instances in which the American people became possessed by irrational fears and yielded, however briefly, to the rantings of demagogues. In the 1840s, Irish Catholics by the thousands came to the United States to settle; native-born workers feared that these newcomers would take their jobs; and there was deep prejudice against Catholics on the part of rigid Protestants. The result of these pressures was a great wave of antiforeign, anti-Catholic agitation that swept the nation. Out of this agitation a political party was born—the Know-Nothing Party with its creed of prejudice and hate. Catholic churches and schools were attacked and burned, and it looked for a brief period of time as if the Know-Nothings would actually take over the country.

So it has gone periodically throughout our history—from the Salem witch hunt in 1692 to the great wave of McCarthyism in the 1950s. Sometimes there were basic wrongs, deep-seated and long-lasting, that played into the hands of the demagogues. But even in these instances the appeal was always to passion, not to reason; and the remedy urged was violence, no matter who was hurt.

Tracing these outbreaks of hysteria, one finds many common features. Perhaps the first lesson we should learn is this: when passion and fear rule the land, no man is safe. He who accuses another winds up himself accused. The Salem madness came to an end only after it had exposed itself, only after the fever had reached a point where even the highest and most distinguished men in the colony were being accused of practicing witchcraft. Similarly, the McCarthy convulsion of the 1950s built up to a final and self-destructive idiocy—the charge that even President Dwight D. Eisenhower, one of the most beloved Americans, had been a secret agent of the Communist conspiracy.

The study of demagoguery teaches other lessons. One is that few men, however intelligent, however good, are immune to the passions of their times. In Massachusetts it was not just the humble and the ignorant, but the best minds and the leaders of the community who began to see witches everywhere. And when they surrendered to such delusions, the first victims became the honest and courageous. In

Salem, those who denied the witchcraft charges were convicted and hanged; those who confessed and offered evidence against others, however dubious their confessions, however untrue their testimony, were protected by the authorities and their lives saved so that they could go on accusing and testifying. This pattern of protecting self-confessed wrong-doers was to be repeated again in the McCarthy era.

Whatever the circumstances, whatever the age, the result is the same: a nation suffers when fear and suspicion get out of hand and when unprincipled men play upon these emotions for their own purposes. When this happens, violence follows, and violence knows no reason; it strikes at all it finds in its path, whether old and weak, whether young and helpless, whether innocent or guilty.

This then is the legacy of the demagogue—a trail of ruined lives, a nation damaged in its very soul. The sickness may pass, but its evil effects often linger on. And the tragedy always is that it never should have happened.

2
THE SALEM WITCH HUNT

The Reverend Samuel Parris was a harsh man in a harsh age. He was pastor of the Puritan church in Salem Village, a town now known as Danvers, Massachusetts. His sermons were concerned with the works of the devil and hell and eternal damnation. Lacking in him was any hint of softness, of that quality known as Christian charity.

There were many ministers like Samuel Parris in those days. To them the devil was very real. He worked his evil magic everywhere. If a child became mysteriously ill—and in those days of limited medical knowledge this was a frequent occurrence—it might be the work of the devil. If a man's cow or horse sickened and died, it could be because some vicious neighbor with dark powers had cast the evil eye upon the creature.

All of this may seem quite silly to us today, but in the late 1600s people accepted the idea that the devil was as real as the parson in his pulpit. He could actually appear before those whom he was tempting to do his evil work. He sometimes carried in his hands a "black book," and in this the names of those who fell under his spell were written in their own blood.

Those who signed this unholy register became witches. They did the devil's will in all things, and the devil promised to protect and reward them. When some major plot was being hatched, the witches held great assemblies called witches' Sabbaths. To these they came from great distances, riding on broomsticks or pokers, or mounted on goats or hogs or dogs, and the devil, in the form of a goat, presided over such meetings while his followers offered him gifts and sacrifices.

All of this was as real to the people of the 1600s as the hearths of home. Few doubted that such things actually happened, and great witch hunts swept all the nations of the civilized world. From one end of Europe to the other, the execution of witches was an almost daily occurrence, and it is estimated that over a period of two-and-a-half centuries more than 300,000 men, women, and children were condemned and put to death for their supposed practicing of witchcraft.

The American colonies, on the whole, had been less afflicted by this madness than the European countries from which the colonists had come. But they had not been wholly free from it. There had been witchcraft cases in Connecticut and in Boston before 1692, but these had been minor events. Not until the devil descended upon Salem Village, not until he began to work his evil spells in the very household of the Reverend Samuel Parris did the solid and sensible colonists take complete leave of their senses.

This Samuel Parris was an embittered man. He had been educated at Harvard Theological School in Boston, but he had left school to make his fortune as a merchant, trading with Barbadoes in the West Indies. Only he hadn't been smart enough to make his fortune; he had made only a business failure. And so he had arrived at the age of thirty-five with little but wreckage in his life—and the need to find a new way of making a living. He decided to become a minister.

Since he had not finished his studies, the better churches
of the Massachusetts Bay Colony were closed to him. The
best offer he could get was that of the church in Salem
Village, a town that was known far and wide as a hornet's
nest. The villagers were among the most quarrelsome in the
colony; the church was divided into factions; and already
two other ministers had been hounded out of town by their
belligerent congregation.

In these circumstances almost any man except Samuel
Parris would have moved cautiously. But Parris, by all the
evidence, was both domineering and grasping; and so, in
his greed, he picked a fight right at the start. He demanded
that the villagers sign over to him full rights to the parsonage and the acreage around it. The congregation, naturally,
wouldn't hear of it. They beat Parris down. Not only did
they refuse to deed him the parsonage, they offered him a
miserly salary and even refused to grant him "the minister's
wood spell"—that is, free firewood for his fireplace. Parris
was going to have to get and chop his own firewood.

Parris, needing a livelihood, finally succumbed and
accepted the severe terms, but with bad grace. He went to
Salem Village determined to teach his flinty parishioners
some lessons. He would not even ordain his deacons until
they had served a probationary period under him. His long
nose sniffed the village for signs of wrongdoing, and he
publicly shamed even some of the leading members of his
church, bringing them to account for the slightest faults.
And so, as often happens to such men, the Reverend Parris
became so busy hunting out the sins of others that he was
blind to what was happening in his own household.

The Parris family was an odd mixture. Parris' wife, a
mousy little woman, colorless in her husband's shadow, ran
about the village, fussing over vague good deeds and leav-

ing the running of her own house largely to two servants. These were part-Negro, part-Indian slaves whom Parris had brought with him from the West Indies. The man, called John Indian, did the heavier chores and sometimes tended bar in Deacon Nathaniel Ingersoll's tavern, across the street from the parsonage. The woman, who was named Tituba, cooked, swept, cleaned—and took care of the two children in the household. These were Parris' daughter, Betty, a golden-haired, meek, nine-year-old who was easily led, and her cousin, Abigail Williams, who was two years older and a far tougher character, with a gift for trouble-making.

Tituba had brought with her from the West Indies some tag ends of voodoo tricks. In the bitter cold winter of 1692, with snow covering the Massachusetts countryside and time hanging heavily on the hands of shut-in children, Tituba began to entertain the two little girls by astonishing them with examples of her magic. Soon the word spread, and older teen-aged girls of the village began to cross the snow-covered fields and enter the Parris kitchen where Tituba wove her spells.

Parris had no idea of what was happening. The first sign that something was wrong appeared in the conduct of little Betty. Earnest and well-behaved, Betty apparently took her father's sermons with the utmost seriousness. The devil was very real to her, and she began to fear that he was kicking up his heels in Tituba's kitchen. She became absent-minded, burst into tears, and sometimes became choked and made hoarse sounds like a barking dog. Alarmed, Parris and his wife lavished all kinds of attention on Betty; and Abigail, seeing this, evidently decided to get some notice for herself. She began to get down on all fours, scuttling under tables, barking and braying, and sometimes going into convulsions.

At first, Parris and his wife tried to hide this scandal in their own household. But villagers were always coming and going to the pastor's house, and it was not long before rumors began to spread. When this happened, several of the older girls who had sneaked into the Parris kitchen to witness Tituba's magic began to join the act.

The key figure in this spreading performance was twelve-year-old Ann Putnam. Ann had had a disturbed childhood. Her mother, after whom she was named, had come to Salem Village some twenty years earlier. The elder Ann's sister, Mary, had been the bride of James Bayley, the first minister of the parish—and one whom the villagers had hounded into exile. Misfortune had piled upon misfortune until the elder Ann's mind had become twisted with bitterness and suspicion.

Her sister, Mary, had borne one child, but the child had soon become ill and died. Then Mary herself had died. Ann had married Sergeant Thomas Putnam. She had given birth to child after child, and all, except the younger Ann, had died. The mother kept seeing the figures of her dead sister and her dead children in her dreams, and she kept passing her own sick fancies on to her little daughter. And so the girl's mind was conditioned to believe in evil spells, the power of the evil eye—in the reality of witchcraft.

As Salem Village began to hum with the half-concealed scandal in the pastor's house, Ann Putnam and her companion, Mercy Lewis, the Putnam's nineteen-year-old maid servant, went into the most horrible convulsions. Their legs became twisted and distorted; their tongues protruded as if they were strangling; and they made hoarse animal sounds.

Those who saw them in such seizures hardly expected them to live, but they did.

In more modern times, some of these symptoms would have been recognized as genuine, though not the work of witchcraft. There are persons who are easily suggestible. They can be made to believe almost anything, and in extreme cases their beliefs drive them into a kind of insanity that produces fits and convulsions. Such people today are called hysterics. But in 1692 there was no such thing as modern psychology, and there seemed to be only one simple and obvious explanation for such afflictions. They were the work of the ever-busy devil. The village doctor examined the stricken girls and was unable, in the limited knowledge of the time, to find any real cause for their sufferings. And so he did what was expected of him; he pronounced the anticipated verdict: "The evil hand is on them."

The Reverend Samuel Parris was just the kind of man to leap at such a conclusion. How else could one explain the upheaval in his own holy household? Obviously, the only answer must be that the devil had invaded the very parsonage, and so Parris called upon his fellow ministers in Essex County to join him in doing battle with the forces of darkness. In late February, 1692, the ministers gathered in Salem Village for a day-long fast and day-long prayers. The result was not happy. Some of the afflicted girls sat staring with vacant eyes while prayers were offered for them; others shrieked and threw fits at every holy word. The star of the show was Abigail Williams. She shrieked, barked, threw herself upon the floor, putting on a performance that left the villagers stunned and wondering what she might do when the next prayer was offered.

Out of all this came the first accusation. Little Betty Parris, most troubled of all the girls, dropped the name of Tituba. Instantly, many things became clear to the narrow-minded villagers. What more natural agent for the devil could there be, the townspeople thought, than this outlandish servant, who was half-Negro, half-Indian? Parris himself had no doubts. He demanded that Tituba tell him the truth. The poor slave tried. She explained that she had been just trying to amuse the children with some innocent tricks, some innocent magic. This was doubtless the truth, but it was not the truth that Parris wanted. Nothing would satisfy him unless Tituba told him a "truth" in line with his beliefs. And so, to get this "truth," he began to beat Tituba. The helpless slave, frightened out of her wits, fearing Parris would beat her to death, broke down and "confessed." She told Parris what he wanted to know. Yes, she said, she *had* practiced witchcraft—and the witch hunt in Salem Village was on.

The first witches named by Tituba were natural targets, the kind of unpopular persons who could be accused with safety. One was Sarah Good, a pipe-smoking, dirty woman with matted gray hair who begged from door to door and who sometimes walked away cursing when she was refused a handout. The other was Sarah Osburne, a well-to-do widow whose first husband had left her a sturdy house with fine oaken paneling. After her husband died, Sarah Osburne had shocked the village by taking into her home as a handyman one William Osburne. She finally got around to marrying him, but great had been the scandal. Perhaps resenting the gossip, Sarah Osburne had not set foot inside church in fourteen months—and that, in Puritan New England, was a deadly sin.

Warrants were issued on February 29, 1692 (this was a leap year) for Tituba, Sarah Good, and Sarah Osburne. Two magistrates came to Salem Village to hold a preliminary hearing. They were John Hathorne, the great-great-grandfather of Nathaniel Hawthorne, one of America's most famous early novelists, and Jonathan Corwin. Hathorne was the stronger personality, and he took virtual command of the hearings, assisted by Samuel Parris, who acted as secretary, taking down testimony and suggesting persons who should be investigated. Hathorne was supposed to be a judge, but with Samuel Parris egging him on, he acted more like a prosecutor. His mind obviously had been made up before the hearings began, and he hammered at the witnesses, dissatisfied with any answers except those that would advance his pursuit of witches.

Tituba, conditioned by Parris' whip, with Parris himself taking down her testimony, knew exactly what was expected of her. Taking the witness stand on March 1, she held Salem Village spellbound for three days. She told of red rats and red cats, and these rats and cats could talk to her. They told her: "Serve me."

Tituba also described a Thing that was "something like a cat"; it had a woman's face, it had wings, and it did Goody Osburne's bidding. There was also "a tall man from Boston" (obviously the devil himself), who had appeared before Tituba. Tituba testified that "he tell me he God and I must believe and serve him six years. . . . The first time I believe him God he was glad."

The devil, Tituba said, sometimes called meetings of his witches—those gatherings known as witches' Sabbaths. She had ridden to such meetings herself, she testified, "upon a stick or pole and Good and Osburne behind me. We ride taking hold of one another; don't know how we go, for I saw no trees nor path, but was presently there."

When she had signed up with the devil, Tituba said, she had made a mark in his book that was "red like blood." She had seen the names of others in the book. Two of the names were those of Sarah Good and Sarah Osburne. There had been nine names in all. At this, a gasp ran through the audience. The villagers had supposed they had just two witches to deal with besides Tituba, but now, they were told, there must be seven others. Who could these others be? Neighbor looked at neighbor, each wondering of the other: Could he (or she) be one of the witches?

There was, of course, no hope for Sarah Good or Sarah Osburne. What good could denials do them set against Tituba's testimony? So they were packed off to jail to await final trial.

The girls who supposedly were victims of the witches were quiet at first as Tituba began to testify. Could it be that they were afraid of what she might say about *them*? As it became clear that they had nothing to fear from Tituba, however, they became more bold. They began to yelp and cry out that they were being pinched and tortured. No one could see that they were being injured, but that did not matter. A key article of the witchcraft delusion held that the devil possessed the power to make the spirits of his witches leave their bodies and do the dark deeds he commanded. No ordinary spectator could see this ghostly activity. Only the victims could. And so few doubted the stories of the "afflicted" girls when they cried out that they were being attacked by the vicious spirits of Good and Osburne.

It took a highly courageous person to make a stand against almost an entire village, led by a fanatical minister and deluded magistrates. Anyone who opposed the frenzy took great risks. But there were a few stout-hearted people who dared.

One was a farmer named John Procter. The maid servant in his home, Mary Warren, had been one of the yelping and crying "afflicted" girls. Procter took stern steps to cure her of her fits. He plopped her down at her spinning wheel and told her to get to work before he took the strap to her hide. This threat seemed to work a miraculous cure on Mary Warren. She threw no more fits—not, at least, until the witch-hunting magistrates, much to Procter's disgust, undid all his good work by coming around and encouraging her to make new accusations.

Two of Procter's neighbors, Giles and Martha Cory, also stoutly disbelieved in witches. Martha was an outspoken woman. She never hesitated to say just what was in her mind, and she was usually right, a circumstance that did not make her dearly beloved by neighbors whom she put in the wrong. When the witch hunt started, Martha Cory made no secret of her feelings. There were, she said, no such things as witches.

Rumors about the way she thought spread through the village, and the result was inevitable. It is necessary in a witch hunt for everyone to believe; if nonbelievers are tolerated, the whole business may go up in a puff of smoke. And so it wasn't long before young Ann Putnam was accusing Martha Cory of being a witch.

"I told you so," said the outspoken Martha, knowing she was no witch and seeing in the charge proof of her convictions.

The trouble is that one may know one is not a witch— but how is one to prove it to others? In Martha Cory's case, she had at first some doubters on her side. Unlike Sarah Osburne, Martha Cory had been a God-fearing woman; she never missed attendance at church. Could it be possible that such a religious woman was really a witch? Some members of the congregation thought Ann Putnam must have made a mistake, and they paid a call on Martha. "I do not believe there are witches," Martha told them bluntly. They were shocked. Not to believe in witches was almost as bad as not believing in God, and the delegation went away, muttering to themselves and shaking their heads.

A warrant was sworn out for Martha Cory's arrest, but since the next day was a Sunday and since a warrant could not be served on the Sabbath in Puritan New England, court action had to wait until Monday. And in the mean-time Martha Cory decided to go to church.

There had never been a church service like that in Salem Village—or anywhere else in New England, for that mat-ter. Deodat Lawson, who had been one of the ministers of the parish before Parris, had returned to preach the ser-mon. Wanting to find out what the witch hunt was about, he had gone to the parsonage on Saturday night to talk with Parris. Hardly had he arrived before Abigail Williams went into her act. She swooped through the rooms as if she were about to take off and fly. She began to cry out that she was being pinched and tortured by a shape no one else could see. Finally, she had darted into the fireplace and had begun to hurl burning brands about the house. It had ap-peared that she was even going to fly up the chimney, had she not been grabbed and hauled to safety.

Deodat Lawson, who had doubted at first, was shocked by this performance. Shaken and hollow-eyed, he took the pulpit the next morning, looked out at his congregation—

and found staring up at him like any other God-fearing woman none other than Martha Cory. The girls saw Martha, too, and they began to shriek and cry, creating such an uproar that Lawson could hardly make himself heard over it. The afternoon service was even worse. There sat stout, determined Martha Cory again—and there were the shrieking, twisting, performing girls.

"Look!" cried Abigail Williams. "There sits Goody Cory on the beam suckling a yellow bird betwixt her fingers."

The congregation looked in horror, but of course saw nothing. Martha still sat right there in their midst, not on any beam; but few doubted that her shape, which only the girls could see, had taken leave of her body and was indeed sitting on the beam with its yellow bird.

"I will open the eyes of the magistrates and the ministers," Martha Cory had said when she was first accused. Foolish woman. She went to her pretrial examination the next day already condemned and convicted in the eyes of the village.

The accusing girls were, of course, in the seats of honor on the front benches. At Martha's appearance, they began to shriek and twist their bodies. Asked who afflicted them, they said in a chorus, "Goody Cory." Asked why she did such things (the question itself showed that her judges assumed she did), Martha replied: "I don't afflict them."

"Who doth?" demanded John Hathorne.

"I do not know. How should I know?" Martha replied, reasonably enough. She added that "we must not believe these distracted children"—a remark that offended Hathorne, who had become so distracted himself that he believed them completely.

The girls began to shriek that Martha Cory, who called

herself "a gospel woman," was instead "a gospel witch."
One pretended to see a Black Man standing beside her and
whispering in her ear. Others heard the sound of a drum;
and, looking out of the meeting house, they swore they
could see witches from all over Essex County gathering on
the very steps for one of their witches' Sabbaths. "Why
don't you go, gospel witch? Why don't you go, too?" they
cried at Martha Cory.

Poor Martha, who had thought that a life of goodness
would speak for her, was undone. How could innocence
stand before such accusations? "You can't prove me a
witch!" Martha cried to the magistrates. But that was not
the point. In a witch hunt, the accused witch is assumed to
be guilty. He must prove that he is *not* a witch—a very
different thing, something almost impossible to prove to
minds already convinced. And so Martha Cory, too, was
led away and clapped into prison to await trial.

Her case made a deep impression on the village. If so
God-fearing a woman was indeed "a gospel witch," who
was safe? Who was innocent? And what about all those
other witches the girls had seen gathering on the very steps
of the meeting house during Martha Cory's trial? The very
size of this reported gathering showed that Essex County
must be crawling with witches, and so, naturally, it became
the duty of every good man to help the magistrates in the
holy task of tracking them down.

Not even the highest and most respectable were now
safe. The witch hunt that had begun, as all such witch
hunts do, by attacking those who were disliked and despised now had built up to a mass insanity. No evidence
could fight it. No reputation could be proof against its
charges. And to be accused was to be convicted.

Nothing showed this better than the case of Rebecca Nurse. Rebecca and her husband, Francis, had founded one of the hardest-working and most respected families in all of Salem Village. They had bought a three-hundred-acre farm with a fine, large main house, and had arranged to pay for the property in twenty yearly installments. Father, sons, and sons-in-law had all labored as one, making those yearly payments and supporting their families. By 1692 they had only six more years to go to clear off the mortgage, and none doubted the thrifty, hard-working family would do it.

At the heart of the family circle was Rebecca Nurse, a wise and gentle woman. She was seventy-one and sick in bed in the winter of 1692 when the younger Ann Putnam first "cried out" on her during the trial of Martha Cory. Abigail Williams had taken up the cry, and the elder Ann Putnam had added to it, naming Rebecca as the witch who had killed her children one by one.

When Rebecca, still ill in bed, was first informed of these charges, she was stunned. "I can say before my eternal father that I am innocent," she said. "I never afflicted no child, no never in my life."

But no denial could save her. On March 23, still feeble from her illness, she was taken before the magistrates. At once, first one girl, then another went into convulsions. They set up such a "hideous screitch and noise" that Deodat Lawson, who had left the meeting house to work on a sermon, heard the hubbub from a considerable distance. Above the outcry rose the shrill, shrewish voice of the elder Ann Putnam.

"Did you not bring the Black Man with you?" she shrieked at Rebecca. "Did you not bid me tempt God and die?"

The weak and aged woman stood there, belabored from all sides, the children howling at her, the elder Ann Putnam accusing her of murder. "Oh, Lord, help me!" Rebecca cried, spreading her hands helplessly. As she did so, the children spread their hands, too, in exact imitation, acting as if Rebecca's spirit were compelling them to move even as she moved.

This and one other circumstance greatly impressed the magistrates. Though Rebecca Nurse protested her innocence, though she appeared on the verge of collapse, she did not weep. This was highly suspicious, for it was a key article of the witchcraft superstition that a witch could not cry. And so the aged, trembling Rebecca Nurse was led off to prison.

Not quite everyone in Salem Village had lost his wits. There were a few rare souls who scorned the universal madness. One such was bold John Procter, the masterful man who had almost jolted his maid servant, Mary Warren, back to her senses. Hearing of the verdict against Rebecca Nurse, Procter snorted that the accusing girls should all be sent to the whipping post. "If they are let alone, we shall all be devils and witches," he said. If anybody was to be hanged, it should not be persons like Rebecca Nurse who had led blameless lives, but the crazed girls who accused them. Hang the girls if hang you must, shouted Procter. Poor, courageous John Procter. He did not realize that the man who defies the witch hunt names himself as one of the next victims of it.

In the brief interval between the jailing of Rebecca Nurse and the filing of charges against John Procter himself, the Reverend Samuel Parris preached a sermon. It was one for which he was never to be forgiven. Rebecca Nurse's family and kin came to despise him because he acted more like a man of hate than a man of God. He showed no pity, no mercy, but pounded along the witch-hunt trail, a fierce and vengeful man seeking new victims. On Sunday, April 3, Parris announced to his congregation that his text would be: "Have I not chosen you twelve and one is a devil?"

Listening to him was Sarah Cloyce, the wife of Peter Cloyce and a much younger sister of Rebecca Nurse. Sarah was already bitter at the treatment Rebecca had received at the hands of Parris and the magistrates, and when Parris proclaimed the witch-hunt theme of his sermon, Sarah rose angrily to her feet, stormed down the aisle and left the church, slamming the door behind her so hard that the rafters rattled.

Salem Village had never before witnessed such defiance of a minister's holy word, and the congregation gasped at Sarah's bold and unheard of act. When the noise created by her exit had died down, Parris continued, almost menacingly:

"Christ knows how many devils there are in his church and who they are."

Sarah Cloyce, by defying Parris and slamming the church door, naturally had signed the warrant for her own arrest. Instantly, she became an accused witch. But she was not alone. Named with her were Elizabeth Procter, John Procter's wife—and, eventually, John himself.

The witch hunt was now getting too big for little Salem Village. And so when the new hearings were held on April 11, they took place in the larger meeting house in Salem Town. The handling of the case was also different. No longer was it just in the hands of local magistrates, but Deputy Governor Thomas Danforth and several members of the General Council of Massachusetts came up from Boston to see what was going on.

The presence of these important persons seemed to subdue the performing girls when Sarah Cloyce faced the magistrates. They were relatively quiet, and Sarah, a spirited woman, might have faced them down had it not been for Tituba's mate, John Indian. He insisted that Sarah had harmed him "a great many times." Sarah called him "a grievous liar." Whereupon John Indian promptly tumbled to the floor in a fit, rolling about and howling with pain.

John Procter had come to the hearing mainly to support his wife, Elizabeth, who had been "cried out on" by some of the girls. He evidently hoped that, with some of the most prominent men in the colony present, common sense would prevail. He could not know that, in a witch hunt, many of the so-called best minds are as gullible as the most hopeless ignoramus. This quickly became clear in the April 11 hearing in Salem Town.

The Procters had been so well liked by their neighbors, they were such solid citizens, that many thought at first the girls must have been mistaken. When Elizabeth took the stand, the girls themselves seemed a little uncertain and eyed her in silence. But there was no holding John Indian.

"There is the woman who came in her shift and choked me!" he cried, pointing an accusing finger at Elizabeth Procter.

This set off the girls, who began to mutter and moan, working themselves up into a frenzy and producing an "awful" din. They cried out that Elizabeth was now sitting on a beam of the meeting house, their favorite perch for witches, and several shrieked that she had tried to get them to sign the Black Book in blood.

The uproar became so loud, with shouts and shrieks and charges flying back and forth, that Parris gave up trying to keep an accurate record of it. John Procter, enraged, tried to shout above the hubbub in defense of his wife, but whatever he said Parris didn't record. Yet Parris could hear and note the screech of Abigail Williams, who turned upon Procter, crying: "Why he can pinch as well as she!"

This was enough to send John Procter off to jail along with his wife and Sarah Cloyce to stand trial for witchcraft.

The arrest of the Procters put their maid servant, Mary Warren, in a decided fix. She was left alone at home to care for the Procters' five children, and the oldest of them were mature enough to know what was going on. They spoke their minds to Mary, telling her just what they thought of her for having had a hand in starting all this witchcraft nonsense.

In addition, Mary soon received another sharp lesson. The laws at the time provided for the seizure of the goods and property of convicted witches. Such seizures were supposed to await the final verdict after trial; but in the Procters' case, a scoundrelly sheriff couldn't wait. He raided the Procter farm and seized everything he could lay his hands on—"all the goods, provision and cattle." He sold some of the cattle for half price, and he killed others and shipped the meat off to the West Indies. He "threw out the beer out of the barrel and carried away the barrel, emptied a pot of broth and took away the pot and left nothing for the support of the children," the youngest of whom were three and seven years old.

There are some indications that Mary Warren worshiped the masterful John Procter, and the mere fact of his arrest, coupled with the greed of the raiding sheriff, shook some sense into her. She began to mutter that the accusing girls were playing an evil game. "It was for sport," one of them had said about the charges against the Procters. And Mary Warren gave it as her opinion that the magistrates who had swallowed whole every tale the girls had told them might as well have listened to the rantings of the insane.

Word of Mary Warren's desertion of the cause soon reached the magistrates—and, of course, the accusing girls. This backsliding by one of their own inner circle obviously posed a threat to everybody, and so there was now demonstrated another feature of a typical witch-hunt frenzy. Anyone who has a change of heart, anyone who tries to tell the truth, thus exposing the falsity of past charges, quickly finds himself accused and in great danger.

Mary Warren was arrested on April 19 on the charge that she had become a witch herself. When she was taken before the magistrates, the girls who had been her playmates and partners in the witch hunt promptly went into their howling, hysterical act. They all pointed their fingers at Mary and denounced her as a witch who was tormenting them.

It was all too much for Mary Warren, a weak-willed girl to begin with. She cried out: "I will speak . . . Oh, I am sorry for it! I am sorry for it! Oh, Lord, help me! Oh, good Lord, save me! I will tell! I will tell!"

What she was sorry for, what she might have told, no one was ever to know. For Mary Warren was suddenly seized with one of her old fits. Her jaws locked. She became speechless. Her body began to twist in convulsions, and she fell down and had to be carried from the hearing room.

It was left to the afflicted girls to explain the meaning of all this to the magistrates. Mary, they said, had been about to reveal the innermost secrets of witchcraft, which she knew because she was herself a witch, and the shapes of Martha Cory and Elizabeth Procter, to keep her from betraying them, had attacked and choked her. Only the girls, of course, had been able to see this ghostly attack; but, take their word for it, this was just what had happened. Having already accepted the idea that only the girls could see such things, the magistrates naturally believed whatever they were told and packed poor Mary Warren off to jail to await trial.

Even then, left to herself, Mary Warren might have told the truth, but she was not, of course, left to herself. The magistrates kept after her every day, pestering her with questions, demanding that she tell them "the truth"—but, of course, only "the truth" they wanted to hear. Mary tried to hold out against them at times. Especially, she struggled to keep from offering evidence against her master, John Procter. But it would have taken a character as courageous as that of Procter himself to stand up against the constant pressure—and Mary was not so strong a person. Finally, on May 12, she gave up and told the magistrates everything that it had been suggested to her they wanted to hear.

Once she had surrendered and gone back to being just a poor girl afflicted by witches, Mary Warren found that everything changed for her. The magistrates were delighted. They released Mary from jail and restored her to her place of honor in the circle of the performing girls. Mary no longer joined in their antics, but she sat there with them and by her mere presence gave support to their charges. The great danger to the witch hunt had passed. One who had attempted to tell the truth had been brought to see the folly of trying to stand alone in the gale of unreason that was sweeping Massachusetts.

The pattern had now been set. Once the highest officials in Massachusetts accepted the idea of spectral evidence—that is, the notion that the devil could separate the spirits of his followers from their bodies and make them perform deeds only those who were attacked could see—there was no chance of stopping the hysteria. The witches whom the girls kept seeing at large witches' Sabbaths must be hunted down. And so person after person was "cried out on," and half-a-dozen suspects a week were packed into the tiny Massachusetts jails.

Among all these new arrests, one stood out—that of a minister.

It began, as so much began, with the younger Ann Putnam and Abigail Williams. On April 20 Ann Putnam pretended to see witches from all over Essex County alighting from their flying rods in Parris' pasture. They stuck their sticks into the ground, and those who came from afar sat down to eat sandwiches. But one figure stood out—that of a minister. Ann cried out—her father said he heard her—"Oh, dreadfull, dreadfull! Here is a minister come! What, are ministers witches too?"

The girl kept pestering this pastor-devil to tell her who he was. "Oh dreadfull, tell me your name that I may know who you are," she cried.

One might have thought that this lieutenant of the devil would have wanted to keep his identity secret, but, no, this was a most obliging servant of darkness. He told Ann just who he was—the Reverend George Burroughs, who had been the pastor in Salem Village some ten years earlier. He was one of those ministers who had found it impossible to get along with his quarrelsome flock, and he had gone off into the wilderness of Maine, where he was living with his third wife and his children when Ann Putnam spotted his shape in Parris' pasture.

Even the witch-hunting magistrates, who had demonstrated their ability to believe almost anything, hesitated to accept the idea that a minister, of all people, could be an agent of the devil. But Abigail Williams didn't give them much time to nourish their doubts.

She put on a performance that topped everything she had done previously. Before a crowd of villagers in front of Ingersoll's tavern, she cried out that she had spotted the menacing shape of the ministerial devil. "There he stands!" she cried, pointing, and Benjamin Hutchinson hurled a pitchfork into the road at the spot. His aim must have been good, for Abigail reported she could hear the minister's greatcoat tear.

Even so close a call could not daunt this devil, however. When the throng went into the meeting room of the tavern to hear a Lecture Day sermon, the ghostly minister thrust his way right in amongst them. Fortunately for little Abigail, Hutchinson had stayed close by her side. He whipped out his sword to protect her and cut and slashed so fiercely that he must have mortally wounded the shape, for Abigail reported that the minister had changed into a gray cat and that Sarah Good had swooped in to pick him up.

The Lecture Day sermon was then delivered, but the excitement wasn't over. Hardly had the service finished when the girls set up an outcry. Shapes of the witches were pouring into the tavern through the windows, thick as horse flies, they cried. The men in the congregation drew their swords, slashing and flailing about them. They must have done great injury to the witches, for the girls declared that the floor was running with blood (though, naturally, this was spectral blood that only the girls could see) and that the witches were fleeing into Parris' pasture. There they paused, mourning their dead.

After such a desperate battle with the army of witches, there could be little doubt about the fate of George Burroughs. A warrant was sworn out for his arrest, and it was served in the most dramatic fashion. Burroughs was just sitting down to dinner in his home in Wells, Maine, one day early in May, 1692, when deputies from Salem strode in, yanked him up from the dinner table and rode off with him.

Burroughs, who had no idea what was happening, found when he arrived in Salem that he was being charged with murder. Ann Putnam declared that the ghostly forms of his first two wives had appeared before her and had told her that Burroughs had killed them. Soldiers of the village who had been killed fighting the Indians had been the victims, Ann declared, not of the Indians—but of Burroughs. The minister had bewitched them to their deaths. Neither Burroughs nor the magistrates, of course, could see the witnesses who told Ann all these details. And there wasn't much chance to cross-examine Ann; for, having given her testimony, she promptly went into a convulsion and had to be carried out. Burroughs' fate was as good as sealed.

With Massachusetts' jails bulging to the bursting point, it became necessary to get final trials under way. Deputy Governor William Stoughton, a tall, silver-haired, impressive man, presided as chief justice. Ordinary people from the villages made up the juries.

The pattern that was to be set quickly became obvious.

Despite his appearance, despite his position, Stoughton was a hard and bigoted man. Mercy was a word unknown to him. Conviction was his goal. This became obvious in the trial of Rebecca Nurse late in June.

The aged woman had been so liked and respected by her neighbors that twenty of them, despite the witch-hunt frenzy, dared to risk their own lives by signing a petition describing her noble character. The trial jury, headed by one Thomas Fisk, was greatly impressed by this. The testifying girls went into their usual crazed antics, howling that Rebecca was torturing them, turning the hearing room into a madhouse.

This performance, new to Stoughton and most of the jurors, must have had a tremendous effect. Yet the common-sense men of the jury under Thomas Fisk were not to be stampeded. They recognized that there was no solid testimony against Rebecca. It all depended upon the visions of the girls, upon fantasy. And so they came in with a surprising verdict—not guilty.

Stoughton was not the man to accept a decision at such odds with his desires. He sent the jury back to consider the error of its ways. And the jurors, overawed perhaps by the position and prestige of the deputy governor, did what was expected of them. They convicted Rebecca.

When even a Rebecca Nurse could be found guilty of witchcraft, there was little hope for anyone else. Trial after trial ended the same way, with the same verdict: guilty.

On a Tuesday, July 19, the first of the executions took place. Five of the convicted witches, including Rebecca Nurse and Sarah Good, were taken out to Gallows Hill behind Salem Village—and there they were hanged. The executions were marked by one memorable incident. Most of the victims went quietly to their deaths, but not Sarah Good. At the foot of the gallows, she turned on the Reverend Nicholas Noyes, another fierce pastor of the Parris stripe. Noyes had appealed to her to save her soul by confessing; she very well knew she was a witch, he said.

"You're a liar!" Sarah screamed at him. "I'm no more a witch than you are a wizard! If you take my life away, God will give you blood to drink."

It was a threat to make a man shudder—and one that would be recalled years later when Noyes did, indeed, die of a hemorrhage.

The bodies of the witches were buried in a shallow grave on Gallows Hill, but that of Rebecca Nurse did not long remain there. In the dark of night, after the executioners and crowds had departed, her loving sons stole up to the grave site, recovered her body, and gave her a quiet and decent burial on their own acres.

The execution of Rebecca Nurse carried with it a meaning that was not lost on others. Here was a woman so saintly, so beloved, that her family and twenty of her neighbors had risked being "cried out on" themselves to stand by her. Yet she had been convicted, her life taken. If this could happen to a woman whose whole life cried out her innocence, what hope was there for others? What chance of changing the minds of judges who believed in one's guilt before any testimony was taken?

There was no hope; there was no chance. There was only one remedy—flight. And so some of the most prominent persons in Massachusetts, finding themselves denounced in the never-ending tales of the girls, fled from the colony and sought refuge in the saner atmosphere of New York.

One of the first to take this route was John Alden, the son of John and Priscilla, the most famous lovers in the early days of the Plymouth Colony. John Alden was a commanding figure in his own right, a sea captain and soldier, a valiant fighter in the Indian wars. He was also "a tall man from Boston," and the witch hunters were fascinated by the possibility that in him they might have found the chief devil of whom Tituba had talked.

When Alden strode into court, the girls, who had never seen him except in their fevered fancies, had some difficulty in picking him out at first. One of them, indeed, identified the wrong man until someone whispered in her ear and pointed out Alden. Thus set straight, the girls had no difficulty thereafter in identifying Alden as the devil himself. When he looked at them, they fell down, shrieking and going into convulsions. When he touched them with his hand at the direction of the judges, they rose up, miraculously cured. It was, said Alden, just a bunch of "juggling tricks"; but his judges, persuaded that their witnesses could tell no lies, took his sword away from him and held him prisoner. John Alden was not, however, the kind of a man to wait meekly to be hanged; and so, one September night, he gave his jailers the slip, burst in upon some friends at midnight, got himself a horse and rode away to New York.

In a similar case, Philip English and his wife, Mary, of Salem, were "cried out on" by the girls. Now the Englishes were one of the most prominent families in the colony. They lived in a fine, large mansion on Essex Street in Salem, and English was one of the wealthiest men in the colony and a friend of the governor, Sir William Phips. Originally a sea captain, English had branched out into business. He owned fourteen buildings, a wharf, and some twenty sailing ships. But even his wealth and position could not save him. His wife was arrested and jailed; so was he. Seeing there was no chance to clear themselves, English and his wife broke out of jail (aided, it was said, by Sir William Phips himself) and fled to safety in New York.

These flights of the prominent and the executions of the poor were writing a lesson that the people of Massachusetts dimly began to understand. If you had friends and influence, you could get out of jail and get away. If you were poor, you went to Gallows Hill.

This last trip was one that was taken on August 19 by five more of the convicted "witches." The batch included the courageous John Procter and the Reverend George Burroughs. Cotton Mather, the most famous divine in all of Massachusetts, rode along to see that the executions were properly carried out, and it was perhaps well for the witch hunters that he did.

At the foot of the scaffold, Burroughs was given a chance to speak, and he addressed the crowd in such simple and effective terms that many began to weep. And then he did something else. Calmly, gravely, he recited the Lord's Prayer.

Now it was another key article of superstition that a witch could not utter such holy words. What, then, was one to make of Burroughs' prayer? Did it not signify he was innocent? The crowd surged forward as if to rescue the minister at the very foot of the ladder. But at this point Cotton Mather, dressed all in black, stood high in his stirrups and spoke in a commanding voice. The devil, he said, was never more devilish than when he appeared as an angel of light. Burroughs must have made a pact with the devil to recite the Lord's Prayer; it was all a trick. The crowd fell back, and Burroughs was hanged.

On and on went the executions. Twenty persons were to

die before the insanity reached its end late in September. Of these one death stood out above all others—that of Giles Cory, the slow-witted, stubborn husband of the outspoken Martha.

When Giles had been accused by the girls, he had stood in court mute. Having seen the futility of offering a defense, he refused to say a word. His judges, of course, could not permit such defiance; Giles must be made to talk. And so on September 19, the sheriff took Giles Cory out to a field near the jail, spread-eagled him upon the ground and began to pile rocks upon his chest. The idea was that, before such a victim would allow his chest to be caved in, he would talk. But the witch hunters had reckoned without the incredible stubbornness and courage of Giles Cory.

Rock after rock was piled on his helpless body, and despite the terrible pain, Giles Cory defied them. He gasped just once, a command—"Pile on!" And that was all they got out of him until finally the weight of the rocks crushed him to death.

Not even so horrible a performance could stir the sympathy of Cotton Mather, Deputy Governor Stoughton, and the other judges. To them, Giles Cory remained just an obstinate old witch. But others began to think. Did pressing a man to death in such horrible fashion really represent justice? If a man were truly guilty, wouldn't he prefer to talk and earn himself at least the swifter death by hanging? What had possessed Giles Cory? They began to wonder— and to doubt.

Three days later, on September 22, eight more victims of the witch hunt, including Martha Cory, made the long trip to Gallows Hill. It was to be the last of the hangings.

Governor Phips, a man of honor and common sense,

had left the handling of the witchcraft business in the hands of Stoughton, his deputy, a better-educated man and one presumably better equipped to deal with such complicated matters. Now, however, a point had been reached at which Phips had to relieve Stoughton and act himself.

The witch hunt, as most witch hunts do, committed the ultimate folly. The girls became carried away with their success. They "cried out" on virtually everyone. They did not know where to stop. And so they finally accused even Lady Phips herself.

This was too much for the governor. He knew, at least, that his own wife was not a witch. And if the charges against her were false, how was anyone to believe the charges against others? Had the colony been hanging innocent persons? The thought was enough to make Phips decide to end the whole business, and so he issued an order that there should be no further arrests and commitments. That did it. Since there were no more arrests, no more trials, suddenly those public performances that had so aroused the people of Massachusetts stopped. Without this constant sensationalism, the witch hunt died, and sanity gradually returned to the villages. But it would be years before Massachusetts would hear the last of it.

Back in Salem Village, the Reverend Samuel Parris—the fanatical religious demagogue who had started it all—was called to account by his angry flock. On April 21, 1693, a group of his parishioners read out to his face a list of charges that said, in effect, that he was no true man of God. They denounced him for "his easy and strong faith and belief" in the charges of the girls; for "his laying aside of . . . charity toward his neighbors"; for his use of "unwarrantable and ungrounded methods for discovering what he was desirous to know" about the accused; and for "his un-safe, unaccountable oath" against several of those accused. They even questioned whether Parris had kept a true record of the testimony given at the trials.

The dispute dragged on for years. Parris apologized to his congregation for any errors he might have committed; the devil, he regretted, must have deceived and made use even of him, a minister. The elders of Salem Village wanted the members of the church to accept the apology— and Parris. But the aroused families of the village—many, like the Nurses, who had lost loved ones in the witch hunt —would have nothing to do with a compromise that, in effect, would forgive Parris. They appealed to the elders of the three Churches of Christ in Boston, asking them to send Parris packing. They accused him of having gone privately to the girls to encourage them in their performances and to drum up charges against persons whom he disliked.

It was obvious that there would be no peace in Salem Village until Parris went, and so finally, in 1697, he was removed from his church and departed the village, a dis-credited man. He left behind him only bitter memories and a phrase, witch hunt, that will be remembered as long as American history is written.

3
THE KNOW-NOTHINGS

The evil that bad men do is to be expected and can be recognized for what it is because one knows that the men are bad. But the evil that the good do is worse. Often it is not recognized, often it parades as principle and high purpose—and is accepted as such because one cannot imagine that its authors would stoop to bad practices.

Yet it was these so-called good men who inflamed passions and touched off the wildest period of demagoguery in American history. It was these "good men" who built the fires of the powerful Know-Nothing movement. The Know-Nothings were members of super-patriotic and super-secret societies, and they were pledged, if questioned about their activities, to reply "I know nothing"—hence, the name for a movement that, for one brief period, seemed about to capture control of the entire American government.

First and foremost among the demagogues of Know-Nothingism was a fiery preacher, the Reverend Lyman Beecher, of Boston. Born in New Haven, Connecticut, on October 12, 1775, Beecher studied at Yale, entered the ministry and became a noted revivalist. He was also the father of famous children. One of his sons, Henry Ward Beecher, became the most popular pulpit orator of his day, and a daughter, Harriet Beecher Stowe, was to write *Uncle Tom's Cabin*—the book that aroused Northern passions against slavery.

Lyman Beecher was the son of a blacksmith, and he had inherited his father's powerful physique. He was a man who liked to be physically active, hoisting dumbbells, shoveling sand, sawing up all the wood in the neighborhood he could find to saw. He was tall, with a deep-cleft chin, and he wore his plentiful hair loose and fluffy, without a part. His thundering voice could drown out a pipe organ. In action in the pulpit, he often became so carried away that his loose hair would fly about and his powerful gesturing arms were apt to knock over anything that got in their way. More than once the scribbled notes for his sermon became the victims of some thrashing blow and fluttered like autumn leaves over the forward members of his congregation. On such occasions, his deacons had to scurry about, gathering up the fallen notes and passing them up to the performer in the pulpit so that he might not lose the trend of his thought.

Such was the man who, in 1830, at the age of fifty-five, came to Boston and declared war on Catholics.

America had a long history of anti-Catholic prejudice to which a demagogue might appeal. The colonists who came here from England carried with them memories of a centuries-long struggle against the power of Spain. They remembered with deep hatred how the Catholic Inquisition had burned Protestants at the stake. These memories were kept alive in the 1700s by more than half a century of colonial wars against the Catholic powers of France and Spain.

The depth of this hatred was shown in the ways it expressed itself. In 1659 Massachusetts passed a law banning the celebration of Christmas on the ground it was a popish festival. During the 1700s a popular New England game was called Break the Pope's Neck, and November 5 was celebrated as Pope's Day—with a parade ending with the burning of an effigy of the Pope.

This deep-rooted hatred of Catholicism and the Pope flamed anew in the 1800s as Irish Catholic immigrants began to come in increasing numbers into the Eastern states. The descendants of the original settlers, overwhelmingly Protestant in their religion, had all the old hates and fears stirred anew by this influx of immigrants professing a faith that Americans believed to be hostile to freedom and democracy. Fears that native-born Americans would be drowned in this tide of foreigners began to spread. The spirit of the times was expressed in a Boston street poster in 1830—the same year in which Lyman Beecher became pastor of the Hanover Street Presbyterian Church. The poster read:

"All Catholics and all persons who favor the Catholic Church are . . . vile imposters, liars, villains, and cowardly cutthroats. A TRUE AMERICAN."

Lyman Beecher had hardly arrived in Boston before he began a series of thundering sermons, denouncing the evils he saw on every hand. He roared against whiskey drinking, though he was suspected of keeping a jug handy himself. He attacked the Unitarians, the liberal Protestants who were rebelling against the harsh code of the Congregational Church. And he flayed Catholics in some of the most inflammatory speeches Boston had ever heard.

Lyman and his son, the Reverend Edward Beecher, who had become pastor of the fashionable Park Street Church, kept up a running fire of oratory against the Catholics. They denounced the Pope as "anti-Christ"; monks were corrupt and nuns immoral. They saw immigrants as the tools of Rome and tyranny. The Irish were "guzzlers of beer and whiskey"; they were responsible for the rising crime rate, and they took jobs right out of the hands of honest American workingmen. Such fierce, unceasing attacks, appealing to passion and hate, soon earned for Beecher's church the nickname of "Brimstone corner."

A special Beecher target was the Ursuline Convent School in an imposing brick building atop Mount Benedict in nearby Charlestown. The Ursuline nuns, who had established the convent in 1818, had built up their school until it was recognized as one of the best in the young nation. The wealthy Episcopalian and Unitarian families of Boston, at war with rigid Congregationalism, sent their sons and daughters there. The school was so good it attracted students from as far away as the Southern states and Canada. It was so good that it became a special object of hate for little men with poisoned minds in the pulpits. They were certain that the Ursulines' purpose was, not education, but the conversion of an entire generation of young Americans to Catholicism.

With Lyman Beecher and his son stoking the fires of hate, it needed only a spark to set all Boston aflame—and it was not as if they had not had ample warning of the violence with which they toyed.

In 1829 a group of native Americans had rioted through the streets of Boston for three days, attacking and stoning the homes of Irish Catholics. In 1833 another riot had broken out. A group of drunken Irishmen had beaten a native American to death in a brawl, and in revenge a mob of five hundred "true-blue Americans" had swarmed through the Irish section, killing people and burning homes. The militia had been called out to prevent such savagery, but it had just stood and watched. Even such eruptions did not cool the fiery zeal of Lyman Beecher. He continued to attack all Catholics; and so, with the aid of a feeble-minded girl, he reaped the inevitable whirlwind.

The girl was Rebecca Theresa Reed, known to most of Charlestown as a dimwit. She had begged the nuns to let her do chores around the convent for six months to prove that she was a proper person to join their order. Unfortunately for all, she quickly proved the very opposite. She was lazy, slovenly, and a born trouble-maker. The nuns put up with her for four months and then turned her out. Rebecca was angry at this treatment, and her anger was vengeful and deadly. Filled with spite, Rebecca got her revenge by making up wild tales about life in the convent. She told how one nun, suffering from brain fever, had been thrown into an underground prison cell. And she declared that she had "escaped" herself just in time to prevent the monks from kidnaping her and spiriting her off into the wilds of Canada.

In a more sane climate, such tales might have been recognized for what they were—the imaginings of a sick mind. But in the Boston that Lyman Beecher and his son had done so much to mold, any wild tale about evil Catholic plots was quickly snapped up and wholly believed.

Chance now played into the hands of the fanatics. The stir created by Rebecca Reed had not had a chance to die down when, on the night of July 28, 1834, an Ursuline nun actually did flee from the convent. She was Elizabeth Harrison, a music teacher. Overwork and long hours of teaching had brought her to the point of a nervous breakdown, and she fled to the home of Edward Cutter, a brick manufacturer. After she had had a chance to rest and calm down, Elizabeth Harrison was shocked at what she had done. "Oh, my God, where were my senses?" she cried. "How can I repair the injury I have done?" She couldn't, though she tried. She returned to the convent of her own free will and insisted that she was happy there. But Boston chose to believe a far different story.

The wildest tales swept the city. Boston papers reported that Elizabeth Harrison's friends had called at the convent to make sure she was all right, "but she was not to be found." The insinuation was that she had been done away with—or shanghaied to Canada in a plot like the one Rebecca Reed had described.

All Boston began to boil with anger, and it was at this point that Lyman Beecher, who had been in the West, popped back into town. On August 9, 1834, a huge rally was held, with crowds shouting, "Down with the convent! Away with the nuns!" The next day was Sunday, the Lord's day, and Lyman Beecher went to work. He tore all around Boston in a perfect frenzy, thundering his message of hate to overflow crowds at four different churches.

The Catholic Church, he roared, "holds now in darkness and bondage nearly half the civilized world." All the most precious American liberties were being threatened by this church, a "most skillful, powerful, dreadful system of corruption." It was a church that reduced to slavery all "those who live under it," and the spread of its influence to America brought with it "ignorance and prejudice, passion and irreligion and crime." Everywhere he spoke, Lyman Beecher's organ voice trumpeted against the Ursuline convent.

The very next day the convent was attacked in one of the most shameful episodes in American history.

On Monday night a mob, led by a well-organized group

of truckmen and bricklayers, marched against the convent. Carrying banners and shouting "No Popery" and "Down with the Cross," they milled about the convent. The nuns and children had been asleep until they were awakened by the ruckus. The mother superior pleaded with the mob to go away, but it had no such intention. Though town officials had been warned in advance, they had sent only one constable to the scene, and he, of course, could do nothing. Tar barrels were set to bubbling in a nearby field; and shortly after midnight, when all was ready, some forty or fifty hard-core ruffians led the attack on the convent. They burst through its front doors as the nuns and some sixty terrified pupils fled out the back. The torch was put to the convent and a nearby farm building that the Ursulines sometimes used as a dormitory; and as both buildings went up in flames, the rioters screamed and capered in the flickering light.

One might have thought that even Lyman Beecher would have been sickened by this devil's work he had so encouraged. But he was not. A demagogue must, by the very nature of his business, be a hypocrite. In his hands, truth becomes untruth, and the lie becomes the holy word.

Lyman Beecher was a perfect example of the breed. The following Sunday, he made a bow to conscience; he deplored mob violence. But then he sought to justify it. Then, and for many years to come, he kept turning the entire situation upside down, picturing the Irish as the rioters and the native Americans as their terrified victims. He charged that Boston had had to live "five nights under arms" in terror of an Irish mob. "The capital of New England had been thrown into consternation" by Catholic threats, he declared. The truth was the very opposite, and well Lyman Beecher must have known it. But in a witch hunt truth is always the enemy. A witch hunt feeds on its myths; it cannot exist without them—and so they must be preserved at all costs.

Perhaps if the American people could have known the real truth about what happened in Boston, they might not have been victims of the kind of mass prejudice and insanity that was to mark the next twenty years. But Lyman Beecher and a host of other highly placed men turned their backs on truth and preserved the myth of the Catholic menace through an unending barrage of propaganda.

Slander became a flourishing national business from which fortunes were made. The story of the Ursuline convent, so twisted in the telling that it bore no relation to truth, served for decades as the basis for the wildest yarns. Rebecca Reed pioneered the field. Early in 1835, doubtless with the help of an obliging ghost writer, she produced *Six Months in a Convent*. The book was pretty tame fare compared to some that were to come later, but so great was the anti-Catholic fever that several thousand copies had been sold by the end of 1835, and the book was being republished throughout the United States and England.

Rebecca's book was followed by one called *Testimony of More Than 100 Witnesses*. This dealt with wild rumors and imaginary tales recounted by members of the mob that had burned the convent. There was no end to the flood of horror stories. As late as 1854, novelist Charles W. Frothingham let his imagination run riot in the plots of three novels, all based upon the idea that virtuous Protestant girls had been kidnaped by sex-starved priests and held prisoners in the dungeons of the convent until rescued by their heroic lovers.

The *Western Monthly Review* commented in June, 1835, that abuse of Catholics had become "a regular trade." The writing and publishing of anti-Catholic books, it noted, was "a part of the regular industry of the country, as much as the making of nutmegs or the construction of clocks." A favorite theme pictured priests as sex-starved maniacs with whom no woman was safe. In developing this theme, nothing was too absurd, nothing too fantastic. One Rosamund Culbertson described her sex life as the mistress of a Cuban priest and charged that priests made a practice of killing young Negro boys and grinding them up into sausages. "Those who bought and eat [*sic*] the sausages say they are the best sausages they ever eat [*sic*]," she wrote.

One might have thought that the better minds of the day would have turned in disgust from such shoddy propaganda; but, no, it was to be as it had been in Salem, as it was to be later in the Communist witch hunt of the 1950s. Many of the so-called leaders of society were either as deluded as the worst elements in it—or they yielded to the irresistible temptation to coin money and gain power by joining the hate brigades.

Among the prime movers in this frenzy of anti-Catholic slop was another minister, the Reverend W. C. Brownlee, of New York. He edited a hate sheet originally called *The Protestant* and later the *American Protestant Vindicator*. It became the official organ of the Protestant Reformation Society, and Brownlee sent his agents all around the country, talking up the Catholic hate campaign. With the stage thus set, Brownlee and a small inner circle of ministerial plotters turned the trick of the decade. They foisted off on the public as fact the wild rantings of another feeble-minded girl, Maria Monk.

When Maria Monk arrived in New York City it was obvious that she was about to have a baby. Her explanation for this state of affairs was that she had been a nun in the Hotel Dieu Convent in Montreal, and there a priest had fathered her unborn child.

Maria Monk's story, jibing as it did with the darkest suspicions of the time, swiftly became the juiciest item of gossip in New York, and it wasn't long before it drew to her bedside a remarkable group. This consisted of a renegade Catholic priest, the Reverend William K. Hoyt, who may well have been Maria's lover; the Reverend J. J. Slocum; the Reverend Arthur Tappan, brother of a famous abolitionist; Theodore Dwight, a Connecticut lawyer and banker; the Reverend George Bourne, a rabble-rousing anti-Catholic—and, of course, the pinch-faced Brownlee.

Slocum wrote most of Maria Monk's story, helped along by suggestions from the others. The tale was certainly sensational enough to curl the hair of anyone dim-witted enough to believe it. According to Maria, she had been raised a Protestant, but had been converted to Catholicism and had joined the Montreal nunnery. She had been told she must "obey the priests in all things"—and she had soon discovered, she said, that this meant literally *all things*. She described a secret underground passageway that, she said, connected the nunnery with a nearby monastery. Priests used this tunnel, she declared, to enter the nunnery and make merry with the nuns. According to Maria, nuns who refused to make love to the priests were executed. Most, however, faced with such a fate, did their duty, and the children born of these affairs were strangled and thrown into a secret pit in the basement. She herself had seen two such babies strangled, Maria asserted; and so, when she found that she was bearing the child of a Father Phelan, she had fled from the nunnery and come to New York.

Having put this vile yarn down on paper, the ministerial conspirators sought a publisher. They turned to James Harper, a partner in the highly respected publishing house of Harper Brothers and himself a leading light of Know-Nothingism. Harper's brothers found Maria's autobiography too gamy for their taste, but they recognized its sales value. And so a dummy firm was set up, headed by a couple of Harper employees, and in January, 1836, Maria's tale was published under the title, *Awful Disclosures of the Hotel Dieu Nunnery of Montreal.* There was hardly a word of truth in it beyond the basic fact that an unmarried woman named Maria Monk was about to have a baby; but Brownlee gave the *Awful Disclosures* a great send-off in the *Vindicator*, and in no time the book swept the nation like wildfire.

Maria Monk's mother, who was still living in Montreal, made her own awful disclosures about her daughter's *Awful Disclosures.* Maria, she said, had never been quite right since she ran a lead pencil into her head as a child. She had been a wild girl, her mother said—so wild, indeed, that she had been confined, not in the nunnery, but in the Catholic Magdalen Asylum for wayward girls in Montreal. Two impartial and skeptical Protestant pastors —there were still some around—were permitted to search the entire Hotel Dieu nunnery from basement to attic, and they reported that Maria obviously had never been in the nunnery because her description of its physical layout was wrong. There was no secret passageway; there was no pit into which strangled babies could be thrown. The whole business of the *Awful Disclosures* was a fraud and a hoax.

This was obvious to sane men then, and it is unquestioned now. But it is an unfortunate fact of life that, once important men have staked their reputations on the truth of a lie, the lie must be made to appear the truth. Brownlee and his demagogic fellow pastors shouted to the heavens that the attacks on Maria Monk were just part of a foul Catholic plot. They brought her into their churches and turned over their pulpits to her. Maria sometimes appeared in nun's costume, with her baby in her arms. She was short, plump, and curvaceous. She had deep-set, little black eyes, a pouting mouth, and not much of a chin. She was, without doubt, cunning and greedy. She relished her notoriety and gladly recited the wild and vicious tale that could be guaranteed to keep her in the public eye.

It is typical of such periods of mass frenzy that no exposure, no finding of fact, can make the least impression on the public mind. The public, once blinded by passion, clings to its delusions. Never was this better illustrated than in the case of Maria Monk. Even the fact that Maria produced a second baby whose father was unknown did not shake the mass faith in her. Maria herself did not claim that this second child was the result of a forced affair with a Catholic priest. Only Brownlee went so far, contending in the *American Protestant Vindicator* that the Jesuits had "arranged" Maria's second pregnancy.

Maria eventually got herself married, but she so wasted her husband's income in drink and wild living that he left her. She was arrested in 1849 for picking the pockets of her male companion of the moment in a New York house of prostitution, and she died in prison shortly afterwards. But her *Awful Disclosures* went marching on. Up to the time of the Civil War, the book had sold some 300,000

copies—an enormous sale for the times and an indication
of the willingness of the public both to read gamy books
and to swallow whole any lie that was printed about the
Catholic Church.

This insanity to which Maria Monk contributed so
much was not just the work of feeble-minded girls and
fanatic Protestant pastors. Joined in the cause were some
highly intelligent men who gave their energies and their
prestige to this devil's work.

One of these was none other than Samuel F. B. Morse,
famous in history as the inventor of the telegraph and the
Morse code. One bright June day in 1830 Morse was in
Rome, watching a papal procession. Suddenly, his hat was
struck from his head by a soldier who, Morse wrote,
cursed and taunted him with "the expression of a demon
in his countenance." This expression became in Morse's
angry mind a symbol for the entire Catholic Church, and
he returned to America seething with hatred for Catholicism.

Taking up his pen, he dashed off two volumes exposing
what he believed to be the Catholic menace. Their titles
pretty well indicated their contents. The first was called
*Foreign Conspiracy Against the Liberties of the United
States*. The second: *Imminent Dangers to the Free Institutions of the United States through Foreign Immigration*.
In these works Morse played to the deepest and darkest
and most irrational fears of his time. There was a "foreign
plot," centered in Rome and Catholicism, to deprive
Americans of their freedom. And this plot was being advanced by the flood of immigrants, composed largely of
followers of Rome.

Morse pictured the West as the scene of danger. The

plotters, he wrote, intended to seize control of the Mississippi Valley and then march with fire and sword on Washington. He screamed in print: "Will you longer be deceived by the pensioned Jesuits who have surrounded your press, are now using it all over the country to stifle cries of danger and lull your fears . . . ? Up! Up! I beseech you, Awake! To your posts! Fly to protect the vulnerable places of our Constitution and laws. Place your guards! You will need them, and quickly, too. And first shut the gates."

In this ranting attack Morse was joined by the Reverend Lyman Beecher. Beecher had gone from Boston to Cincinnati to head Lane Seminary. His purpose was to battle the Catholic "plot" to "seize" the West, and he was so hipped on this one idea that he forbade all discussion of what was becoming the most heated issue of the day—slavery. This so aroused his students that the majority of them walked out and founded a new college, Oberlin.

Not even such a demonstration that he was becoming out of touch with his times could swerve Lyman Beecher from his purpose. In 1835 he published his *Plea for the West*, a book that raved less than Morse's but was devoted to exposing the same menace. Nearly all immigrants, according to Beecher, were "agents of Rome." They came here to try "to stamp out American republicanism." They were an ignorant rabble that could not be educated and Americanized. They were stupid tools in the hands of wily Jesuit priests intent upon destroying all our free institutions.

There was, of course, hardly a word of truth in any of it. The facts and figures were plain. Less than one-fifth of all immigrants coming here at the time were Catholics.

One great wave of immigrants consisted of Germans, and most were Lutherans or Free Thinkers even more hostile to the Catholic Church than Lyman Beecher. Nor were they dumb, ignorant clods. A great percentage of them were educated persons, as was demonstrated by the fact that, by 1851, they had established some one hundred and fifty German-language newspapers, all opposing slavery and advocating political and social reforms. Most of the Irish immigrants were, of course, Catholics. But they came to America not as the result of any Catholic plot, but to escape poverty and tyranny in their homeland. As an Edinburgh newspaper reported, "the one great cause" for their coming was "the desire for political and religious freedom." The newspaper added that it was "the young, the restless and the imaginative" who went to America seeking "for the ideal freedom."

This was the reality, but the demagogues swamped all America with their delusions. Morse and Beecher had scores of imitators; and newspapers, periodicals, books flooded the nation with wild and imaginative tales about the great Catholic plot to seize the West and march on Washington.

No demagogue or group of demagogues can play with this kind of dynamite for years without touching off in the end a violent and bloody explosion. In this era of Know-Nothingism, the eruption came in Philadelphia in the spring of 1844. The American Bible Society, a Protestant group, had begun a campaign to place the Protestant version of the Scriptures in every schoolroom. When teachers began to read from the Protestant Bibles, the Catholics protested, tempers flared—and rioting followed.

A proclamation published on May 6, 1844, summoned

all native Americans to a rally to be held that afternoon in
Kensington, an Irish suburb of Philadelphia. All good
Americans were called upon to uphold their rights
"against the assaults of Aliens and Foreigners." Several
thousand, responding to this call, marched through
drenching rain to the Market House, directly across the
street from the Hibernia Hose Company. Shooting broke
out. Who started it could never be discovered, but two
men were killed—George Shiffler, one of the marchers,
and Patrick Fisher, an Irishman.

"On, On Americans! Liberty or death!" shouted a gray-
haired nativist as the shots rang out.

But brawny Irish laborers poured out of the firehouse,
charged the marchers—and the heroic, native-born Americans fled.

They soon regained their courage, however. Massing in
even larger numbers that very night, they returned to the
Kensington district and destroyed the homes of several
Irish families before the militia scattered them. It was only
the beginning.

The next day excited crowds surged through the streets
of the City of Brotherly Love. They gathered on almost
every street corner, listening to speakers who ranted and
raved against the Catholics. A torn American flag was
displayed. On it were printed these words: "This is the flag
that was trampled underfoot by the Irish papists." Two
Irishmen, recognized as among the leaders in the previous
day's fighting, were seized, and the mob marched them to
the mayor's house, shouting: "Kill them! Kill them! Blood
for blood!"

The editor of the *Native American*, a local newspaper,
went almost out of his mind. He edged his columns with

black borders—and called for more bloodshed. "The
bloody hand of the Pope has stretched itself forth to our
destruction," he raved. "We now call on our fellow-citi-
zens . . . to arm."

Inflamed, a huge Protestant mob stormed once more
into Kensington. This time they demolished the Hibernia
firehouse. They burned thirty homes. The militia, late in
arriving, finally broke up the riot, but all Philadelphia was
now seething with hate and a thirst for still more violence.

The next day, the third day of the riots, was the worst of
all. Once more a huge mob attacked the Kensington district. Within a few hours, whole blocks of Irish homes had
been put to the torch. With flames leaping to the skies
behind them, the rioters next assaulted the Catholic
churches. St. Michael's was first. Its priest, donning a hasty
disguise, fled out the back as the mob charged through the
front doors and set the church afire. St. Augustine's was
next. The mayor, summoned from his daughter's birthday
party, arrived in time to try to save the church. Standing
on the front steps, he pleaded with the mob. But the mob
roared right over him, trampling him underfoot, and soon
St. Augustine's was also in flames.

Even the rabble-rousers who had been responsible for all
this were appalled at the fruits of their labors. One editor
asked: "Who would not give worlds to wipe off the foul
blot from the disgraced name of our city?" And even the
editor of the *Native American*, he who had issued the call
to arms, declared himself shocked and revolted by the
burning of churches.

But it is easier to arouse the passions of a mob than to
cool them, and for days roving bands continued to loot and

burn. A convent and other Catholic properties and homes were reduced to ashes, and there were more deaths on both sides.

Even so, the worst appeared to be over. But the Native Americans could not let matters rest. On July 4 they staged a huge demonstration in memory of the mob members who had been killed in the Kensington fighting. A crowd estimated at 70,000 paraded through the streets. Tempers blazed again—and more violence followed.

On July 5 a mob marched against Saint Philip de Neri Church. A quantity of arms and ammunition had been stored in the church for defense after the first two Catholic churches had been burned. The arrival of a militia company foiled the plans of the rioters to attack the church, but the next day they were back in larger force than before. By this time, however, an all-Irish militia company known as the Hibernian Greens had been stationed around the church; and when the rioters surged forward, they heard the command given, loud and clear: "Shoot to kill!" That was enough. The mob fled. But one rioter, a former Congressman, Charles Naylor, was seized and held by the Hibernian Greens.

The arrest of Naylor infuriated the self-styled American patriots. On July 7, a Sunday, they returned with two cannons obtained from ships in the harbor and trained the guns on the church doors. But the powder was wet, and the guns would not fire. Obtaining a huge log as a battering ram, the rioters smashed down the church doors and surged inside, only to be brought to a halt by the leveled rifles of the Hibernian Greens. Courage oozed away as the attackers looked into those gun muzzles, and there was much milling around for hours.

An army company arrived on the scene. It threw up barricades around the church and mounted cannon to sweep the streets. But minute by minute the mob swelled in size. A second army company, marching to the aid of the first, was attacked in nearby streets and fired on the rioters. Three were killed and many wounded.

The sounds of battle infuriated the mob around the church. Dry powder had now been obtained, and the two ship cannons were fired point-blank into the ranks of the militiamen guarding the church doors. The soldiers returned the fire, and for hours cannons roared and rifles blazed in the battle of Saint Philip de Neri Church. It was not until a third army company arrived and seized the rioters' cannon that peace was restored. Then it was discovered that two soldiers and twelve civilians had been killed in the fighting, and scores had been wounded.

This was the true story of the Philadelphia riots. There is no disputing the facts. Only Irish homes were burned. Only Catholic churches and convents were set ablaze. And certainly Irish Catholics were not the ones who fired two cannons at one of their own churches. But to admit such truths would be to admit the wrong of the holy cause—and this the super-patriots could never do.

It was not long, therefore, before Congressman Lewis G. Levin was thundering on the floor of the House of Representatives in Washington: "Drilled bands of armed foreigners rushed with impetuous fury upon Native Americans who carried no weapons but, in the majesty of freemen, stood armed only with moral power." It must have been the first time in history that moral power materialized into cannon.

Politicians, of course, sometimes have a great knack of

turning truth upside down, but they were not the only ones to keep alive the myth that poor, home-bred Americans had been attacked by a bunch of bloody foreigners in Philadelphia. Persons with brains and talent were just as blind and wrong-headed.

Take, for example, Anna Ella Carroll, of Maryland. Anna Carroll was a brilliant woman who, within a few years, was to develop much of the grand strategy that won the Civil War. But Anna Carroll at this time was a passionate Know-Nothing, and in 1856 she published a book, *The Great American Battle*. It was 365 pages long, and every page sang a song of hatred for Catholics and foreigners. Writing of the Revolutionary War period, she exclaimed: "Why, these foreigners, these Jesuits, would have chained Washington if they could and strung the necks of patriots like beads." As for the Philadelphia riots, they represented "the butchery of Americans, perpetrated . . . by the Irish Jesuits. . . ."

There was, it seemed, no end to the hysteria—no limit to the fairy tales millions of Americans would swallow as holy truth. With passions aroused by such distortions of fact, it was inevitable that violence should break out in city after city, though none of these outbreaks equaled the bloody turmoil that had shaken the City of Brotherly Love. And it was inevitable, too, with a public stirred to such frenzies, that Know-Nothingism should go into politics.

There are always unscrupulous men, power-grabbing men who will ride such tides of insanity in the hope of seizing fame and fortune for themselves. Sometimes, swept along by their own selfish desires, such men delude themselves and become as fanatical as their following. Sometimes they merely give lip service to the passions of the moment. Who can ever know—perhaps they do not know themselves—where conviction ends and calculation begins? Only one thing is certain: some of the most powerful men and most prominent names of their times are always to be found caught up in such movements.

When Know-Nothingism went political, it lured some highly respectable backing. As early as 1835 it ventured into the city elections in New York with a ticket headed by James Monroe, the nephew of the fifth President of the United States. A leading backer was probably Alexander Hamilton, Jr. And novelist James Fenimore Cooper— famous in early American letters as the author of *The Last of the Mohicans* and other frontier tales—lent his prestige to the movement by denouncing all foreigners as drunkards. The Native Americans lost this election, electing only one assemblyman in Brooklyn, but they did roll up a large vote. They had just begun.

In 1843 the American Republican Party was formed in a blacksmith shop in New York. In the fall elections, though the new party put up unknown and untried men, it nevertheless polled 27 per cent of the total vote. According to one historian of the times, "the wealth, talent and respectability of the community" had joined the Know-Nothing ranks.

The following year—the same year of the Philadelphia riots—this kind of support made itself felt. The Know-Nothings put up a ticket headed by James Harper for mayor. They campaigned against the corruptions of the Democratic machine in New York City; they were aided by a new flood of propaganda and the aroused emotions of the day. And the result was that they swept the city, electing Harper and gaining full control of both branches of the city council. It was just the first of many triumphs to come.

The Mexican War and the first rumblings of the slavery issue turned the attention of the nation away from the anti-Catholic, anti-foreign campaign in the late 1840s. The Know-Nothing movement ebbed like the tide of the sea, but by the early 1850s it came roaring back in full flood, stronger and more threatening than ever.

The Catholics themselves helped this revival of their enemies. Archbishop John Hughes, of New York, made an incredible speech and was so proud of it that he had it widely circulated. It was entitled "The Decline of Protestanism and Its Cause." In this the archbishop proclaimed as official church policy the very things that the Know-Nothings had been accusing Catholics of for years. The mission of Catholicism, he said, was "to convert the world —including the inhabitants of the United States—the people of the cities and the people of the country . . . the Senate, the Cabinet, the President, and all!"

This was folly at its worst. In addition, Catholics in a dozen states began to clamor that a portion of public tax money should be spent for the support of their parochial schools. No wonder many Americans who had been sitting on the sidelines began to think that the Know-Nothings must have been right all along.

Such growing conviction was reinforced by the tensions caused by a great new wave of immigration. A potato famine in Ireland and the failure of the 1848 revolution in Germany sent new hordes fleeing to America. These newcomers were destitute when they left their homelands; and they arrived, most of them, with nothing but the clothes on their backs. They herded into the cities. They grabbed any jobs they could get, working for starvation wages, under-cutting the pay scales of native Americans. They became a hard-drinking, brawling element of the population. "They bring the grog shops like the frogs of Egypt upon us," one temperance writer complained.

Relief rolls swelled. In 1850 one out of every 32 aliens was a pauper receiving public support. Among native Americans, the ratio was only one in 260. Massachusetts spent nearly $400,000 a year to care for the poor, and many towns in the state were being driven to the brink of bankruptcy. Poverty, the surge of foreigners into a strange environment, the herding together in the slums brought what they always bring—crime. In 1850, though aliens made up only 11 per cent of the total population, they committed more than half of the crimes for which 27,000 persons were convicted. "America," one writer declared, "has become the sewer into which the pollutions of Euro-pean jails are emptied."

Patriotic societies sprang up across the land thicker than fleas on a dog's back. The most important was founded by a little-known New Yorker, Charles B. Allen, and was called the Supreme Order of the Star-Spangled Banner. Members had to be native Americans of Anglo-Saxon stock. They could not be Catholics; they could not even have Catholics among their immediate relatives or in-laws. They were pledged to vote for non-Catholics, and they took an oath never to reveal the secrets of the organi-zation. If they were questioned by the curious, they were to reply, "I know nothing"—the saying that came to rep-resent the entire hate movement of decades.

Allen was soon edged out of control of his secret order

by a more powerful man, James W. Barker, a former dry-goods merchant who, it was charged, had burned down his own establishment to collect insurance. Barker, who became known as "The King of Know-Nothingism," was a stodgy and humorless man. On the platform, he shouted, ranted, stomped, and shook his clenched fists to the heavens. After he seized control of the Supreme Order of the Star-Spangled Banner, he began to organize chapters far and wide, through all the states of the East, the West, and the South. The political arm of his secret order became known as the American (or Know-Nothing) Party.

There were other influential shakers and movers behind the scenes. Among the most important was George (Live Oak) Law—the nickname came from his personal political clubs known as Live Oak Clubs—one of the most powerful magnates of his time, a rival of the great Commodore Vanderbilt. Law headed the Dry Dock Bank. He owned streetcar lines in New York City, the Staten Island ferry, the Harlem and Mohawk railroads; and he had sixteen vessels flying his flag on the high seas. Stocky, powerfully built, he had a swollen, oversized head crowned by a great mane of wavy hair. He had a hawk nose and a tight, grim mouth. He was a hard-driving, ruthless man, consumed by personal hates and passions—and ambition. All he wanted was to be President.

Such were the powers who hid behind the mumbo-jumbo of their secret order and fueled the fires of hate. The Know-Nothings were grown-up men playing like juveniles with all the mummery of secret hand grips, secret passwords, secret phrases of recognition, and signals of distress. They were summoned to meetings by the distribution of heart-shaped bits of white paper. If some danger

threatened and the meeting was urgent, the paper was red.
They took for their symbol a mythical figure called "Sam,"
and in 1853 and 1854 newspapers marveled at the manner in which "Sam" was bestriding the land. "He passes
rivers at a bound, scales mountains at a leap, and through
swamp and forest he never loses his way," one writer en-
thused.

It did not seem to matter that where "Sam" leaped
havoc followed. His huge strides across the land re-created
again in all its horror the bloody turmoil of 1844. The
year 1854 saw a riot in the German quarter of Louisville,
Kentucky—an outbreak long remembered as Bloody
Monday—that left twenty dead and hundreds wounded.
Some 1,500 "true-blue Americans" stormed the Irish
quarter in Lawrence, Massachusetts, and left churches
and homes in smoking ruins. Nuns were insulted and attacked on the streets of several cities and had to be rescued by police. In Philadelphia, Baltimore, Boston, and
New Orleans, the strife approached full-scale civil war,
and in St. Louis rioting wiped out virtually every saloon in
the Irish section.

The frenzy carried over at the polls. The Know-Nothings adopted the tactic of taking the major parties by surprise. Often, the names of their candidates did not even
appear upon the ballot; often, they were not disclosed
until the very morning of election day, when the names of
the chosen were passed out to voters on slips of paper.
This strategy of secret and sudden assault shook up the old-
line political machines and delighted voters who relished
the idea of giving corrupt political bosses their comeup-
pance.

The results were startling. In the spring elections of

1854, whole tickets that were not even on the ballots were swept into local offices. Men who had been running without opposition on the morning of election day discovered in the night that they had been defeated by some unknown Know-Nothing of whom they had never heard. Exulting over these victories, the Know-Nothings gathered their forces for an all-out fall campaign.

The catch-phrase name of their organization swept the nation. Know-Nothing candy was sold. There was Know-Nothing Tea. And even Know-Nothing Toothpicks. A clipper ship launched in New York in 1854 was named the *Know-Nothing*. Know-Nothingism was the rage of the day, and the fever was reflected in the ballot box.

Know-Nothings swept Massachusetts and Delaware; by combining with the Whigs, they carried Pennsylvania. Throughout the Northern and border states, winners on the Democratic ticket were secret Know-Nothings, and in all some seventy-five Congressmen were sent to Washington pledged to war on the Pope and Catholicism.

The elections of 1855 saw even more sweeping victories. The Know-Nothings captured Rhode Island, New Hampshire, and Connecticut. They won Maryland and Kentucky among the border states and missed taking Tennessee by a hair's breadth. In New York, Pennsylvania, and California, successful candidates were mainly Know-Nothings. Even in the South, where the party had been slow to organize, Know-Nothings nearly carried Virginia, Georgia, Alabama, Mississippi, and Louisiana, and they did elect some minor officials in Texas.

So sensational were the Know-Nothings' triumphs that politicians conceded the party almost certainly would elect the next President of the United States in 1856. But it was

not to be. Just as swiftly and sensationally as the Know-
Nothing tide had flooded the ballot box, it turned and
ebbed away—and, in the short space of a single year, it all
but disappeared.

The reason for the collapse that was as amazing as the
victories was that the Know-Nothings splintered and fell
apart on the one great issue of their time—slavery. The
party tried to keep both its Northern and Southern wings.
It tried to weasel. But sentiment in the nation was harden-
ing about two extremes. People were either for slavery—
or against it. Not even a magician could find a compromise that would keep both extremes together in a single
party. And the Know-Nothings were no magicians.

They had proved themselves, once elected, incompetent
politicians. They were bigots who could ride to office on
gales of hate and passion; but once in office they did not
know what to do. Some of their state administrations were
scandalously incompetent, and their large delegation in
Congress could not get action on a single Know-Nothing
measure, not even on such a popular step as the limiting of
immigration.

Internal dissension split the party further. The George
Law and James Barker factions fell out over the issue of
Law's presidential ambitions. The Know-Nothing convention in Philadelphia in 1856 finally nominated former
President Millard Fillmore, one of the weakest of all our
Presidents and a man noted for his sympathy for the
South. Anna Carroll was in raptures. She wrote of "the
nationwide sympathy, the rapturous devotion with which
the name of Millard Fillmore came, free from solicitation,
unblemished by cunning, or wrinkled by selfishness, as the
anchor hope of the American Party . . ."

The phrase was apt, for Millard Fillmore plunged like an anchor to a muddy bottom. True, he polled 800,000 votes, 21.7 per cent of the total, but he carried only one state—Anna Carroll's Maryland. The new antislavery Republican Party and the old Democratic Party were left as the two solid political forces in the nation, and Know-Nothingism as a political force was dead.

But the movement that had climaxed a quarter-century of hate-peddling had written its name into American history. And it had coined words and phrases that live on unchanged in extremist movements today. Some of them are easily recognizable. The Know-Nothings had marched to riot under the slogan, "For God and Country"—still a favorite of the American radical right. And they had called themselves, just as super-patriots do today, the only "true Americans" or "true-blue Americans." So deluded, they had burned churches and convents and homes, trampling underfoot the most precious ideals of Americanism. They had been, as historian Carleton Beals has written, "America's first fascist movement." Unfortunately, they were not to be its last.

4
DEMAGOGUES OF THE CIVIL WAR

The most tragic war in American history, the Civil War, set brother against brother, section against section, as the nation writhed over a moral issue that still concerns it—that of the role of the black man in America. It was a time of harsh breaks with traditions of centuries past, a time of inflamed passions—and so a time for demagogues, both North and South.

The wild words of wild men struck sparks against each other, and in an amazingly short period of time an issue which the nation had ignored for centuries became the issue that literally tore the nation apart. Many of the great Americans of the past like Thomas Jefferson had felt that slavery was evil and morally wrong, but it had been so firmly established by centuries of custom that virtually no man in public life felt free to attack it.

Northerners as well as Southerners had owned slaves; many Northern fortunes had been built on the slave trade with Africa. In time, the increasing industrialization of the North made slavery economically impracticable there, but even well into the 1830s there was no great moral revulsion or indignation about it. Northern businessmen traded with Southern plantation owners to the profit of both, and the financial establishment of the time saw no reason to rock the boat. It remained, then, for the masters of passions, both North and South—for those who were in the beginning far-out rebels and extremists—to seize upon the issue and heat it to a point beyond which no compromise was possible.

The first and most notable among those who lit the fuse in the North was William Lloyd Garrison, one of the most unusual demagogues in American history. Garrison was a tall, gaunt man, completely bald, with large eyes set behind rimless glasses. In his personal dealings and conversations, he was charming, mild, and reasonable; but when he set pen to paper or took to the public platform, he gave vent to thoughts that sizzled with passion.

All his life Garrison was motivated by a determination to be noticed, to be heard. He was born in Newburyport, Massachusetts, in December, 1805. His father was a sailor, and a drunkard, who finally deserted his wife, leaving her with three children under seven to support. All of Garrison's boyhood and youth was shadowed by this circumstance. Newburyport had proud mansions, the homes of wealthy merchant princes of the day, and as a boy, Garrison had to visit some of them to get leftover table scraps passed out the kitchen door.

He was placed in the home of foster parents, had to work to help support *their* family, ran away, and was found twenty miles from home by a mail-coach driver, who brought him back to Newburyport. He worked at odd jobs, was apprenticed to a shoemaker and a cabinetmaker —and was a failure at everything until, at the age of thirteen, he wound up in the printing shop of the Newburyport *Herald*. With the smell of printer's ink, he knew that he had found his profession.

Garrison had practically no formal education. Whatever he learned, he gained from his own reading and from the knowledge of current events that came to him while setting type for articles in the *Herald*. Journalism for him was a means of expression, of satisfying a frustrated ego.

There followed years of batting around from job to job, editing one small paper after another. The record of these years, confirmed by the later events in Garrison's life, would seem to say that he had decided he could never climb from the wrong side of the tracks to equality with the wealthy in those Newburyport mansions; he could get ahead, he could attract attention to himself only by being explosively and violently against things most other persons favored. He was against drinking. He was against smoking. In time, he was to be against athletic contests. He was to urge the abolition of international boat races as a great reform. He was to become an anarchist—against all government. He toyed with all of these causes at one time or another, but the one great and consuming cause to which he devoted most of his vast energy was opposition to slavery.

He called for immediate abolition of slavery at a time when the great bulk of Northern citizens were not worrying their heads about it. There was shock value in this extreme position. It made him a challenging figure of his times, and so put him on the road to fame. He became known as an antislavery zealot, and his fierce denunciations of slavery aroused so much opposition that, on occasion, his very life was threatened. A less determined man might have been intimidated, but Garrison reveled in personal danger. It was, perhaps, a tribute to his importance. His writings are filled with expressed longings to become a martyr. He even on one occasion compared himself to Christ and his disciples who had been "buffeted, calumniated and crucified."

Such was the man who, on January 1, 1831, published the first edition of a four-page news sheet called *The Liberator*. Staid Boston at first paid little attention, but Garrison expressed his purpose in the kind of violent prose that, with constant repetition, would ultimately force the entire nation to listen. He wrote:

"I am aware, that many object to the severity of my language; but is there not cause for severity? I *will be* as harsh as truth, and as uncompromising as justice. On this subject I do not wish to think, or speak, or write with moderation . . . I am in earnest—I will not equivocate—I will not excuse—I will not retreat a single inch—AND I WILL BE HEARD."

In this first issue of *The Liberator*, Garrison called attention to an incendiary pamphlet entitled *Walker's Appeal*, which had been written by a free Negro named David Walker, who was running a second-hand clothing business in Boston. Walker had traveled through the South, had seen the degradation and misery of the Negro slaves, and in 1829 had published his pamphlet calling for a slave revolt in the South if slave owners would not grant emancipation. His *Appeal* ran through three editions, each more violent in tone than the one preceding it.

Garrison himself throughout his career preached the creed of nonviolence, but his actions sometimes clashed with his professions. Though he advocated peaceful measures to achieve change, he often defended those who adopted violent tactics and, indeed, seemed at times to relish the results of violence. Furthermore, his inflammatory language in *The Liberator* seemed to incite violence. This advocate of nonviolence wrote so violently that he not only became a hated man in the South, but also was viewed by many principled Northern abolitionists—men like Lewis Tappan, who gave financial support to anti-slavery causes for decades—as a dangerous extremist with whom they did not wish to associate.

These conflicting sides of Garrison seldom showed more clearly than in his treatment of *Walker's Appeal*. Not only did he devote an editorial in his first issue to the *Appeal*, but in subsequent issues he ran three page-one reviews of the pamphlet, all highly complimentary. If the slaves rose up and killed their masters, he wrote, they were not to blame—the American people were. "Our guilty country-men are the ones who put arguments into the mouths, and swords into the hands of slaves," he wrote. "Every sentence that they write—every word that they speak—every resistance that they make . . . is a call upon their slaves to destroy them."

Garrison had hardly finished writing this before violence erupted in the South. In Virginia, a slave named Nat Turner came to believe that he had a holy mission to lead the slaves in the slaughter of the whites. In August, 1831, Turner and a small band of followers killed and mutilated thirteen men, eighteen women, and twenty-four children. They bathed themselves in the blood of their victims as if performing a holy rite.

The massacre sent a wave of terror and outrage through the entire South. White masters living on widely separated plantations had been haunted for generations by the fear that the blacks might rise up and turn upon them in bloody retribution. Now it had happened. And the white reaction was predictable. Nat Turner's followers were hunted down and slaughtered without mercy.

Garrison's reaction to this horrible event was to welcome it. His nonviolent idealism surrendered to the ecstasy of a prophet who had been proved right by events. On September 3, 1831, in an editorial in *The Liberator*, he emphasized on the one hand how strongly he had urged the slaves to be patient and nonviolent, but on the other he seemed almost to exult in the bloody deeds of Nat Turner and his followers. The slaughter of women and children and the mutilation of their bodies brought from him no words of condemnation. He wrote: "The first step of the earthquake, which is ultimately to shake down the fabric of oppression, leaving not one stone upon the other, has been made. The first drops of blood, which are but the prelude to a deluge from the gathering clouds, have fallen." He wrote: "Cast no reproach upon the conduct of the slaves, but let your lips and cheeks bear the blisters of condemnation!" What mattered was the fulfillment of his own dire prophecies in the previous January. He wrote: "What was poetry—imagination—in January, is now a bloody reality. 'Woe to the innocent babe—to mother and daughter!' Is it not true? Turn again to the record of slaughter! Whole families have been cut off—not a mother, not a daughter, not a babe left. Dreadful retaliation! 'The dead bodies of the white and black lying just as they were slain, unburied'—the oppressor and the oppressed equal at last in death—what a spectacle!"

Garrison covered every detail of the Nat Turner rebellion in succeeding issues of *The Liberator*. He described the uprising, the manner in which it was crushed, how Turner was captured, his lengthy confession, his coura-

geous bearing as he went to his execution. This journal-
istic barrage shocked the South almost as much as the
massacre had. Southern propagandists began to blame
Garrison for Nat Turner's rebellion. Garrison's flaunting
of *Walker's Appeal* had inflamed the slaves and caused the
uprising, they cried. This was simply not true. The evidence seems conclusive that Nat Turner had never seen
The Liberator and had never read *Walker's Appeal*, but
the South would not believe it. Though *The Liberator* had
little circulation in the Southern states, it exchanged copies
with about one hundred papers there, and many Southern
editors picked up and reprinted Garrison's most vitriolic
comments. In this way, the delusion grew and spread
throughout the South that Garrison's reaction was the reaction of the North; Garrison, in Southern eyes, was
quickly magnified into a colossal figure several times his
own true stature. Southerners thought he was typical of
Northern abolitionists—typical, indeed, of almost the
whole North—whereas he actually represented only himself and a small handful of extremist followers.

In fact, as late as 1835, the North was so little aroused
about the slavery issue that most of its citizens looked
upon Garrison and his followers as persons a bit touched
in the head. The moral issue had as yet made no impact
upon the average man; he did not really care. And the
business and establishment classes, having important
stakes in the existing system, were opposed to anything
that would disturb it—and so were violently anti-Garri-
son.

The mood of Boston was expressed on August 21,
1835, when the elite of the city filed into Faneuil Hall to
hear a series of speakers denounce the abolitionists. Garri-

son was horrified that this famous meeting place, where the fathers of the Revolution had voiced their ideals, should be used for such a "vile" purpose. The great "Cradle of Liberty," he thundered, had become "the Coffin of Liberty."

The leading businessmen of Boston were in no mood to listen to such attacks. On September 10 a huge gallows with maple beams five inches in diameter was erected in front of Garrison's house. Throngs of the curious came to inspect it until the city fathers finally had it carted away and sawed up for firewood. The gallows, however, had been a warning of real violence to come.

On October 14, 1835, the Boston Female Anti-Slavery Society—a tiny group of women who had been fired up by Garrison's rhetoric—scheduled a meeting in Anti-Slavery Hall at 46 Washington Street. Rumors spread through Boston that the noted British abolitionist, George Thompson, was to speak. Actually, Thompson was not even in Boston, but this made no difference to some of the "better" elements intent on fomenting trouble.

Two prominent merchants who had been among the leaders in the earlier Faneuil Hall meeting secured the printing and distribution of a handbill denouncing Thompson as an "infamous foreign scoundrel" and urging all true patriots to break up the meeting. "A purse of $100 has been raised by a number of patriotic citizens to reward the individual who shall first lay violent hands on Thompson, so that he may be brought to the tar kettle before dark," the handbill announced.

As a result, a mob gathered in front of the hall and surged into the meeting room when some fifteen to twenty women of the antislavery society gathered for their 2 P.M.

session. Thompson, of course, was not present—but Garrison was. "That's Garrison!" the gathered toughs muttered as the abolitionist leader pressed his way through their ranks and took a seat. Calmly, Garrison surveyed the scowling faces. When the mob showed no disposition to leave, he rose and told them:

"Gentlemen, perhaps you are not aware that this is a meeting of the Boston *Female* Anti-Slavery Society, called and intended exclusively for *ladies*, and those only who have been invited to address them. Understanding this fact you will not be so rude or indecorous as to thrust your presence upon this meeting. If, gentlemen, some of you are *ladies*—in disguise—why only apprise me of the fact, give me your names and I will introduce you to the rest of your sex, and you can take seats among them accordingly."

The angry mob was momentarily dumbfounded. Garrison took advantage of the lull to withdraw to his next-door office while the antislavery society tried to conduct their meeting. But Garrison's cool handling of the situation soon gave rise to anger. Realizing how they had been bested, the leaders of the mob became more furious than ever, and they attacked Garrison's office door, kicking in the bottom panel with a resounding crash.

As tempers flared out of control, the pompous, ineffectual mayor of Boston, Theodore Lyman, who had been warned about the trouble in advance and had done nothing to prevent it, appeared upon the scene and urged the antislavery women to cut short their meeting and leave while they had a chance. The spunky women upbraided the mayor, charging that some of his own business friends had promoted the disturbance, but finally they took his advice and left. Only Garrison remained to draw the mounting fury of the mob.

Friends persuaded him to flee out the back window of his office. He dropped to the roof of a shed, lowered himself into Wilson's Lane less than a block from City Hall, dashed into a nearby carpenter's shop, and tried to hide behind a pile of boards on the second floor. The mob, however, had spotted him, and shouts went up:

"Garrison! Garrison! Out with him! Lynch him!"

The rioters pounced upon Garrison, dragged him from his hiding place, tied a rope around his body and forced him to climb down a ladder to the ground. They were about to make off with him when the unexpected happened. Three brawny men thrust their way through the crowd, grabbed his arms and hustled him along with them, shouting: "You shan't hurt him! Don't hurt him! He's an American!"

Garrison, still in one piece though his clothes were shredded, was whisked by these rescuers into the mayor's office in City Hall. Here a hasty conference was held, and it was decided to spirit Garrison for safekeeping into a cell of the Leverett Street Jail. The mob tried to overturn the carriage as Garrison was taken away, but policemen beat them off and got him through. In his jail cell, when friends came to visit him, Garrison was amazingly calm; indeed, he was almost elated. His reaction, it was evident, stemmed not just from relief at his escape, but from satisfaction in his near martyrdom. Time and again in his writings, he had expressed a willingness, almost a desire, to be martyred for his cause; and now it had nearly happened— and the eyes of all Boston had been focused upon him.

After a sound night's sleep, he inscribed on the walls of

his cell a memorial to himself. William Lloyd Garrison, he wrote, had been confined there "to save him from the violence of a 'respectable and influential' mob, who sought to destroy him for preaching the abominable and dangerous doctrine, that all men are created equal. . . ."

His reaction illustrated one of the driving forces of the man. As even one of his admiring biographers has written: "As a boy he had been ignored by his family and humiliated by poverty. More recently, his several failures as editor had brought renewed frustration. Now, however, he was no longer alone and no longer frustrated." All Boston knew him, and it came to him as something of a disappointment, when he first ventured out upon Boston streets some weeks later, that no one seemed to recognize him. He had thought that almost every passerby would realize who he was.

This failure of instant recognition was only a minor irritant, however. Fame had come to Garrison. The attack upon him by his enemies, the outburst of violence in Boston, had achieved the very result that violence usually achieves in America. It was futile and self-defeating. Garrison, the intended victim, became Garrison, the hero of the hour. The circulation of *The Liberator* jumped, and new recruits, shocked by the riot, joined the abolitionist cause. The most notable of these newcomers was Wendell Phillips, a young lawyer, who wondered why his militia regiment had not been called out to shoot down the rioters. Phillips was to become as passionate an abolitionist as Garrison himself, and the two of them came to represent to the South a wild and irrational and utterly hostile North.

Wild, Garrison certainly was—so wild that he often

drove more moderate and stable antislavery leaders out of the abolitionist movement. Here, summarized, are some of the stands he took during the next twenty-five years:

He proclaimed on the masthead of *The Liberator*: "The United States Constitution is 'a covenant with death, and an agreement with hell!' "

He burned copies of the Constitution in public in symbolic protest against a document that he viewed as a pact with the slave interests.

He urged his followers to shun all political activity; he declared he thought it "a sin" to vote.

He cried: "I disown the American flag as the symbol of unequalled hypocrisy and transcendent oppression."

He called for the disruption of the Union: "*The North must separate from the South*, and organize her own institutions on a sure basis."

And finally, in 1859, when John Brown raided Harpers Ferry in an effort to promote a slave uprising in the South, Garrison, the preacher of nonviolence, delivered a eulogy, comparing Brown to the heroes of the Revolution. Those who would condemn Brown as a bloodthirsty fanatic, he cried, "are dangerous members of the community; they are those in whom the love of liberty has died out; they are the lineal descendants of the Tories of the Revolution, only a great deal worse. If the spirit of '76 prevailed today, as it did in that period, it would make the soil of the Commonwealth too hot to hold them."

Little wonder that the South, living always in dread of another and worse Nat Turner rebellion, saw in Garrison and the tremendous uproar he raised the face of a hate-filled and hostile North. Yet the South's understanding, nurtured by its own demagogues using Garrison's outcries to play upon fear, was false. Even the crucial election of 1860, which saw the triumph of Abraham Lincoln and his so-called Black Republicans, was not a triumph for the abolitionist movement. Lincoln, in fact, was far too mild a man for Garrison's liking. Lincoln had no intention of freeing the slaves. He had no intention of interfering with the South's "peculiar institution" of slavery in the states where it already existed. He was opposed to the further extension of slavery into new territories and states; he was determined to preserve the Union, to keep the nation whole. But that was as far as he went. It would take two years of bitter warfare to bring him to issue the Emancipation Proclamation.

The South, however, had been brainwashed beyond the bounds of reason. Thirty years of Garrison's demagoguery in the North had been matched by a corresponding demagoguery in the South. Southern orators held up to their people the image of wild, ranting abolitionists as representative of the entire North; and increasingly they advocated, just as Garrison did, the division of the Union. Only, where Garrison wanted to take the North out of the Union to free it of the sin of slavery, the Southern demagogues wanted the South to secede to preserve a way of life built on slave labor.

The Prince of the Fire-Eaters, as he was called, was William Lowndes Yancey, of Alabama. He was the supreme orator of the South, the man who took the wildest utterances of Garrison and Phillips and portrayed them to his followers as representative of Northern public opinion.

Yancey was born in South Carolina in 1814. His father, a brilliant lawyer, was the partner of John C. Calhoun, the

fierce Southern champion of state's rights. When Yancey
was only three, his father contracted malaria and died at
the age of thirty-four. Mrs. Yancey subsequently married
a Northern minister, and the family went to live in Troy,
New York. Yancey's stepfather had several friends who
were active in the early antislavery movements; the boy
himself was sent to finish his education at Williams College in Massachusetts—but none of this Northern upbring-
ing seems to have had any effect upon him, or perhaps it
had a reverse effect. In any event, he returned to the
South, a youth not yet twenty, and began to study law in
the office of B. F. Perry, later governor of Georgia.

Yancey at this time was five feet ten, slimly built, with
fair skin and a clean-shaven face. His eyes were a dark
and flashing blue; his hair, light brown. When he spoke, he
held himself erect in a commanding pose and used few
gestures. He could speak for an hour at a time without
notes, the words pouring forth as from some inner foun-
tain with never a pause. Although his speech was rapid as
if the words had to rush to keep up with his thoughts, his
voice was clear and ringing, every word was distinct. And
from his earliest days he had the orator's gift; he knew
how to let that magic voice range up and down the scale,
sinking to a penetrating whisper, rising to a thunderous
roar.

Oddly enough, Yancey first made his mark as an ardent
Unionist. South Carolina under the leadership of Calhoun
made the first gestures toward secession in the early
1830s. At this point, slavery was not the issue but a ruin-
ously high tariff that enriched Northern manufacturers at
the expense of the South, whose economy depended entirely upon agriculture. A protective tariff on manufac-

tured goods that ranged up to 45 per cent meant that the South had to pay just that much more for all such goods that it had to buy from abroad or from the North. Calhoun argued that a state or a section so unjustly treated had the right to nullify federal laws and go its own way. President Andrew Jackson replied with the threat to send in troops if South Carolina tried it, and the issue was at length settled when Congress passed a more sensible tariff act. But the idea that a state, if it felt itself wronged, had the right to walk out of the Union had been deeply implanted in the minds of Southerners and was not to go away.

Yancey, who would ride this states' rights gale in later life, was on the opposite side of the fence during the nullification battle of 1834. His hero at the time was Andrew Jackson, and he exerted all his youthful eloquence in upholding Jackson's stand against nullification. He pointed to the old men, veterans of the Revolution, as those who should be respected, whose work should not be undone. A heckler asked him: "Will you fight for the land of your birth?" He answered: "Where liberty is, there is my country." If South Carolina became the advocate of anarchy, he said, he for one would not follow her lead.

This was the man who, in less than ten years, was to become his section's foremost advocate of anarchy. The change came slowly at first, but in the end it made Yancey's the voice of extremism most often heard and heeded in the South.

In 1835, when Yancey was twenty-one, he married the daughter of a wealthy plantation owner, who came to him with a farm and thirty-five slaves as a dowry. Yancey has sometimes been described as a great plantation owner, but this is incorrect. His slave-owning experience was brief, tragic, and costly. His overseer became involved in a feud with the overseer of a neighboring estate; the latter poisoned a well, Yancey's slaves drank the water, and many died. Others were so ill they could not work. Yancey had to turn to newspaper editing and the law to support his sick slaves and make a living for his family.

He remained during the first years of his marriage a stout Unionist, and this led to another tragedy. In September, 1838, he rode to a militia muster twelve miles from Greenville, South Carolina. Afterwards, there was a debate between a leading nullification candidate and a Unionist. Yancey made a pro-Union remark, and Elias Earle, a cousin of his wife and a nullification hothead, insulted him. Yancey boxed his ears. Young Earle lashed at him with a riding whip. Then the crowd parted them.

Several days later, Dr. Robinson N. Earle, the father of Elias, encountered Yancey on the porch of a grain store in Greenville. He attacked Yancey with a grain cradle, slashing at him with the sharp-pointed tines. Yancey's hat was knocked off, the front of his shirt ripped open, and he was driven to the edge of the porch. Here he whipped out a pistol, fired, and killed his wife's uncle. Such were the passions political differences aroused in the South.

Yancey was tried, convicted of manslaughter, fined $1,000, and sentenced to a year in jail. The governor, however, remitted two-thirds of the fine and suspended the sentence; and so Yancey returned to his wife and family.

He later moved his law practice to Montgomery, Alabama, and he soon became a powerful political figure in that state. His oratory made him famous. Most of his speeches were delivered in the open air, with Yancey standing on a rough plank platform erected under the trees. When it was announced that he was to speak, the hills and dales for miles around would empty as their residents flocked to the meeting place, there to marvel at the words that soared and thundered from his lips.

The campaign of 1840, when Yancey was just twenty-six, seems to have marked the beginning of the great change—the complete turnabout that was to transform the defender of the Union into the demagogue who would do more than any other to tear it apart. By now, the South had been shaken by Nat Turner's bloody rebellion, and it had been inflamed by the outcries of Garrison. It had begun to see the North as all pro-Garrison—and its enemy. Yancey threw himself into the campaign as the supporter of the Democratic candidate, President Martin Van Buren, the successor to Andrew Jackson. The Whig Party had nominated a hero of the Indian wars, General William Henry Harrison, and Yancey saw Harrison's candidacy as part of a Northern abolitionist plot against the South.

This was a complete misreading of the facts of the times. The Whigs represented the wealthy and professional classes in the North and the great plantation owners in the South. These leading classes in both sections agreed on one vital point: they wanted a stable federal government that would permit them to continue doing business together. To the business leaders of the North no less than to those of the South, Garrison and his abolitionists were little better than madmen, but already this was a truth the masses of the South had difficulty in seeing. With Yancey's help, Van Buren carried Alabama, but he was to go down to defeat in the nation.

Two years later, Yancey himself was elected to the

Alabama State Senate. He still retained from the days of his youth a lingering hero worship for Andrew Jackson— an emotion that led to a clash illustrative of Yancey's high-flying oratory. Senator Andrew Dougherty, a Whig, declared that he "despised the character of Andrew Jackson as a statesman; the Muscovy drake cannot fly in the wake of the eagle."

Yancey, indignant, jumped to his feet and flashed back:

"True, never was the soaring eagle in his pride of place hawked at and brought low by the mousing owl. In the heaven of his fame, bathed in the sun's glittering effulgence, he still clearly makes his splendid gyrations, unscathed by the missiles of his impotent foes, and far, very far, above the reach of imbecile party malignity."

It is little wonder that the man who could take off in such a florid flight on the spur of the moment was a living marvel to his Southern audiences.

Following his term in the Alabama Senate, Yancey was elected to Congress. He was to serve only one two-year term, but that was enough to make him known in Washington in the mid-1840s as the most extreme of Southern proslavery agitators. Yancey shocked the North by proposing that the slave trade with Africa be reopened and legalized. Appealing to the poorest elements of the South, he cried that enough slaves should be brought in so that every white man, however poor, city dweller or hillbilly, could own at least one. He taunted the North, declaring that its factories were depending on a cheap pool of immigrant labor from Ireland and Northern Europe while the South was denied the right to bring more slaves from Africa. "If it is right to buy slaves in Virginia and carry them to New Orleans," he cried in one speech, "why is it not right to buy them in Cuba, Brazil or Africa?" If the South was to be denied the right to bring in more slaves, Yancey shouted, then he was ready (just as ready as William Lloyd Garrison) to tear up the Constitution and destroy the Union.

His stand was so extreme that even politicians of the South, the more responsible of them, at least, were stirred to fury. Thomas L. Clingman, of North Carolina, was so enraged he challenged Yancey to a duel. They met, fired several shots at each other—all of which missed—and, honor satisfied, returned to the halls of Congress.

Yancey went back to Alabama, and there, for the next fifteen years, he worked tirelessly toward one end—the disruption of the Union and the establishment of a separate Southern state founded on slavery. He would accept no compromise. Compromise was weakness, he thundered; the South's cause was holy. In rising demagogic accents, he urged the South to dedicate itself to honor, patriotism, duty, sacrifice—and, if necessary, war.

The issue that was to set off the demagogues North and South like so many exploding firecrackers now developed. The nation had acquired great new territories in the West as a result of the Mexican War from 1846-48, and the burning question arose: What was to be done with them? Would the new states carved from these territories be slave or free?

The South was already frightened by the increasing power of the North. Northern factories, cities, population, wealth were growing at a pace that were making these so-called free states ever more powerful in comparison with the South. Southern politicians foresaw the day when the admission of more "free states" from the new territories would further diminish their power and influence; and so they clamored for the right to introduce slavery in the new lands. If a Southern plantation owner moved west into Kansas or Nebraska, taking his slaves with him, he must be protected in his "property"—that is, his slaves—by all the power of the national government, the South argued. It did not matter that the new territories were not suited to the kind of vast cotton and tobacco plantations on which slaves were used in the South; the South wanted desperately, however unreasonably and at whatever cost, to extend the boundaries of slavery. On the other hand, the North, increasingly aroused by Garrison and his followers to the inhumanity and brutality of slavery—and, furthermore, having no use for slaves itself—wanted to call a halt. Let the slaves remain in the Southern states where they already were, the North reasoned, but let there be no extension of an essentially immoral system into new and unspoiled territories.

In 1850, these hostile views threatened to tear the nation apart. War was avoided only by the last skillful compromise of the great Kentuckian, Senator Henry Clay. Clay's compromise of 1850 proposed in essence that California be admitted to the Union as a free state; that the rest of the vast tract secured from Mexico should be organized into territorial governments, with Congress taking no stand one way or the other on the slavery issue in these sections; and that Congress, as a sop to the South, should pass a strong Fugitive Slave Act, guaranteeing the return of runaway slaves to their owners.

Nine slaveholding states held a convention in Nashville on June 3 to discuss these proposals. Yancey was there, and Yancey was against compromise of any kind. He argued that, if Clay's bill should pass Congress, the Southern states should secede immediately from the Union. He was supported by another fire-eater from the South, Robert Barnwell Rhett, of South Carolina, but the two of them stood alone. The Nashville convention was ruled by moderates, and they, like most of the people of the nation, sighed with relief when Clay's compromise was adopted.

Not so the passionate Yancey. When the Southern Rights Association wanted to make him a candidate for Congress in 1851, he spurned its support, writing in angry contempt:

"If we cannot live in peace in the Union with the Northern States, it is preferable to go out of it—and when we are beyond the reach of their legislation we may, perhaps, be able to live at peace with them out of the union. Then, I think, the sense of the masses will perceive there can be but one issue made: to wit: *secession or submission.* If you submit, behave like submissionists. Be quiet and peaceable, subservient to the will of your masters. If you resist at all, resist effectually and manfully, use swords, not pins, cannon and iron balls, not paper pellets."

Yancey wanted war. Like Garrison, he had no use for politics and would have no part of it until, nine years later, he got the showdown for which he hungered.

In those brief nine years, the whole fabric of the Union tore apart. The great generation of statesmen who had preserved the Union at all costs—a generation notable for Henry Clay and Daniel Webster—was dying out, and their successors were lesser men, fired more by the passions of their times than by the old ideal of one great, free, indivisible nation. The leader of the Northern Democrats in this new era was Senator Stephen A. Douglas, the so-called Little Giant of Illinois; and it was Douglas who helped to rip the compromise of 1850 apart by introducing his Kansas-Nebraska Bill. Instead of letting the slavery issue rest in quiet peace, where Clay had tried to bury it, Douglas stirred up all the old fires by providing that two territories be created out of the recently acquired Mexican holdings—and that the people in the territories should vote to decide whether they should be slave or free. The South, which wanted a flat congressional protection for slaveholding interests, was outraged.

The hate stirred up by demagogues on both sides mounted swiftly. Harriet Beecher Stowe wrote *Uncle Tom's Cabin*, a novel that portrayed the brutality of the slave system. The book swept the North like wildfire, and the language of the Northern abolitionists became ever more violent. One pamphlet, among scores that Yancey and his followers picked up and flaunted to arouse the passions of the South, fumed on in this way:

"Our plan is to land military forces in the Southern States, who shall raise the standard of freedom and call the slaves to it. . . . One plan is to make war openly and secretly . . . upon the property of the slaveholders and their abettors. . . . Teach the slaves to burn their masters' buildings, to kill the cattle and hogs, to conceal and destroy utensils, to abandon labor in seedtime and harvest, and let the crops perish. To make slaveholders the objects of derision and contempt by flogging them whenever they shall be guilty of flogging their slaves."

This was the kind of advice that could lead only to bloody racial war; the kind of madness that violent John Brown translated into action, first in raids against Southern settlers in Kansas, finally in his attempt to stir up a

slave revolt in his attack on Harpers Ferry. Moderate men
both North and South—Abraham Lincoln, who was to
become President, and Jefferson Davis, who was soon to
lead the new Confederacy—wanted to avert the final tragedy, but they could no longer control the course of events.
Passion was the plaything of the fire-eaters, and passion
now ruled.

The crisis came at the Democratic National Convention
in Charleston, South Carolina, in 1860. The Democratic
Party had long been the dominant party of the nation, and
the nation's stability depended in great degree on its stability. The rising new Republican Party, first tested in the
Presidential election of 1856, was an exclusively Northern
party, backed by many antislavery and abolitionist elements, and the South looked with horror upon the possibility that its nominee might become President. There was
only one way to prevent it. There was only one Democrat
who stood a chance of being elected—Stephen A. Douglas, the "Little Giant." The arithmetic was simple enough
to be understood by any schoolboy in the lower grades. It
required only 152 votes in the electoral college to choose a
President. If the South and the border states remained
solidly in the Democratic column as they had in the past,
Douglas could count on 120 votes from these states alone;
he would need only another 32 in the North and North-
west to win. Almost certainly, he could get them; just as
certainly, no other Democrat could.

But the South was now berserk, and Yancey was the
Pied Piper who led it into madness. He spoke and spoke
and spoke; and wherever he went, huge crowds turned out
to welcome him. His message was clear and hard.

"It is not uncommon to hear those who hold my opinions denounced as agitators," he said in one speech. "I, for one, accept the appellation . . . The prophets of old were agitators . . . If we have the right on our side, it is our bounden duty to agitate."

Having thus put himself on the side of the prophets of the Lord, Yancey prodded and pushed the Alabama legislature into actions that fell just short of a declaration of war. In advance of the Charleston convention, the legislature passed a series of fire-spitting resolutions. It denounced "a sectional party calling itself Republican" that had "acquired the ascendancy in nearly every Northern State and hopes, by success in the approaching Presidential election, to seize the government itself." To permit this "would be an act of suicidal folly and madness." The legislature saw the possibility of "invasion and subversion by the Vandal Hordes of Black Republicanism," and it ordered the state militia reorganized and appropriated $200,000 for "military contingencies." Here was preparation for war before the need for war had been determined.

Such was the mood of Alabama and of much of the South when the Democrats assembled in Charleston's Institute Hall on Monday, April 23, 1860. From the outset, there was little doubt about the identity of the man who would dominate the convention. Murat Halstead, a wise Cincinnati editor, was on the scene, and he noted that the big news of the day on April 20 was the arrival of Yancey.

"He is the man said to be charged with a three-days' speech against Douglas," Halstead wrote. "He is a compact, middle-sized man, straight limbed, with a square-built head and face, and an eye full of expression. He is mild and bland in manner—and has an air of perfect sincerity."

Halstead noted that, despite Yancey's deceptively mild manner, his purpose was reported to be "to precipitate the cotton States into revolution, dissolve the Union, and build up a Southern empire." The mild manner concealing the iron purpose impressed Halstead. "I very much doubt whether the Douglas men have a leader to cope with him in the coming fight," he wrote. And he was right.

The Douglas strategy was to adopt a platform first, then to pick the candidate. The result was a convention battle that lasted for days, frayed tempers, and set one wing of the party against the other. Douglas wanted to dodge the slavery issue by declaring the problem of slavery in the territories should be left to the courts to decide. The Southerners insisted on a flat declaration that slavery would be protected—and from this they would not retreat.

Throughout the early stages of the fierce debate, Yancey sat in the Alabama delegation, calm and unmoved like a disinterested spectator. Yet everyone in the hall, everyone in the packed galleries, knew that he would be the man to hurl the final bombshell. On the fifth day of the convention, the moment came.

The Douglas faction had forced the platform committee to adopt its slavery plank. Northern delegates pleaded with the South to accept this compromise. Do not, they urged, destroy the party, for this would only insure the election of a "Black Republican." The time had come to answer them. Yancey rose to speak. Instantly, the hall rocked with partisan applause. Ladies in the gallery showered him with flowers. Thousands massed on the streets outside added their voices to the uproar, cheering on the champion they could not see or hear.

For an hour and a half, as night descended outside the

hall, Yancey held the floor. He spoke as always, without notes. He spoke, this time, with few of those flowery flourishes at which he was so skilled. He spoke plainly, bluntly, presenting the North with a take-it-or-leave-it ultimatum.

He reviewed the differences between the sections on the slavery issue. He cited the defeats Democrats had suffered in state and congressional elections in the Northern states —and he completely misread the reasons for those defeats. They had been brought about, he said, because the party in the North had tried to appease the antislavery forces. The Northern wing of the party "had not come up to the high ground that must be taken on this subject, in order to defend the South—namely, that slavery was *right.*"

Yancey insisted that neither he nor the members of the Alabama delegation wanted to break up the Union, but the Northern Democrats must understand that the South stood on bedrock—its position that slavery was *right*, it must be protected. A breathless hush hung over Institute Hall as he came, quietly, to his final, fatal, eloquent passage:

"Ours is the property invaded. Ours are the institutions which are at stake; ours is the peace that is to be destroyed; ours is the property that is to be destroyed; ours is the honor at stake—the honor of children, the honor of families, the lives, perhaps, of all—all of which rests upon what your course may ultimately make a great heaving volcano of passion and crime, if you are enabled to consummate your designs. Bear with us then, if we stand sternly here upon what is yet that dormant volcano, and say we yield no position here until we are convinced we are wrong."

He was finished. He sat down. "The speech of Mr. Yancey had been the speech of the convention," Halstead wrote. He reported that the Southerners in the galleries greeted the speech "with rapturous enthusiasm," and that, as Yancey made his points, he was applauded "as if his hearers had been made to stamp and shout by the simultaneous action of electricity."

George A. Pugh, a Douglas Democrat from Ohio, answered Yancey. Like Yancey, he reviewed the party's troubles in the North; but, unlike Yancey, he assigned to them their proper cause. The party had lost favor in the North, he said, because it had worn itself out trying to reach some reasonable compromise, trying to protect the interests of the South. Now Northern Democrats like himself had been told by the foremost spokesman for the South that, in effect, they must hide their faces and eat dirt.

"Gentlemen of the South," Pugh said, "you mistake us —you mistake us—we will not do it."

That did it. The floor of the convention hall turned into bedlam. Halstead described the scene of "a hundred delegates upon the floor, and upon chairs, screaming like panthers, and gesticulating like monkeys." The din was so loud "not a word was audible." The chairman pounded his gavel until it almost broke, trying to restore order, but though one could see the gavel rising and falling, it could not be heard. A crowd of delegates gathered around the chairman "and some seemed to menace him. The delegates gathered in groups and grappled with each other, and surged about like the waves of the sea." Finally, the convention adjourned, but no adjournment, no secret talks and pleadings, could put back together the party that had been ripped so violently apart.

The final, dramatic scene came on Monday, April 30,

just a week after the opening of the convention. The Douglas forces had enough votes to pass their slavery-dodging plank; and, when they did, Yancey rose from his seat, the entire Alabama delegation rose with him—and they walked out. Just before this happened, Halstead wrote, Yancey caught his eye "and he was smiling as any bridegroom. He had evidently made up his mind. He was not perplexed by saucy doubts and fears."

Nor were the other Southerners. Delegation after delegation rose and followed Alabama's lead—Mississippi, Louisiana, South Carolina, Georgia, Virginia, they all went. The convention was a shambles.

That night, on the streets of Charleston, crowds went wild with joy. Halstead wrote that there was a feeling like the Fourth of July, a spirit of jubilee. In front of the courthouse, huge crowds blocked the street, and "a thousand throats called, 'Yancey, Yancey!' "

The Prince of Fire-Eaters appeared and spoke. He was proud and happy, he said, that the South had taken "so proud a position in defense of her Constitutional rights." Scornfully, he called the Democrats left behind in Institute Hall "the Rump Convention." The Southern walkout, assembling nearby, represented the true "Constitutional Democratic Convention," he said. Even now, he told the crowd, perhaps "the pen of the historian was nibbled to write the story of a new Revolution." Halstead, who observed this scene, added: "At this point, some one of the crowd cried, 'Three cheers for the Independent Southern Republic.' They were given with a will."

Yancey and his Southern fire-eaters, by splintering the Democratic Party, had insured the election of Abraham Lincoln and the "Black Republicans" they so hated and feared. They had made the Civil War inevitable.

The Southern states brought on the conflict by seceding and electing Jefferson Davis their President. It was perhaps noteworthy that the South, which had been whipped into a froth by Yancey, turned for leadership to a more moderate man, one who had hoped up to the last moment that rupture and war could be avoided. Yancey, in fact, met with no favor from Jefferson Davis; he was shunted aside, his work done.

But before he left the center of the stage, he coined his most famous phrase, one that has been used time and again, applied to other men in other times and places. Introducing the new President Davis to cheering throngs in the streets of Montgomery, Alabama, Yancey uttered the immortal line: "The man and the hour have met."

It was a sentence that might have been applied more accurately to Yancey himself on that dark spring evening when he rose in Institute Hall and delivered the speech that tore apart the Union.

5

THE LOUISIANA KINGFISH

America has had one demagogue who became a dictator. He was Huey P. Long, the Louisiana Kingfish, and he ruled his state with the kind of iron hand Russian dictator Joseph Stalin would have appreciated.

Huey Long burst upon the American scene in the late 1920s. He soared from obscurity to fame like a streaking rocket—and, like a rocket, he crashed. But in his few short years at the pinnacle, he wielded dictatorial power as no other American politician ever had. He demonstrated that it can happen here; that this democratic land can yield to a power-mad dictator, his greedy followers, and his armed retinue.

Perhaps it could only have happened in Louisiana, and perhaps it only happened there because the very forces that hated Huey Long most passionately were those that made Huey Long possible. Big business and ultraconservative interests had ruled Louisiana like some feudal fiefdom ever since the Civil War era. The owners of large plantations, major oil companies like Standard Oil, old aristocratic families of French descent combined with a corrupt political machine in New Orleans to run the state for their own self-interest. The great mass of the people did not get even the few crumbs that sometimes fall from the tables of the mighty.

A few statistics spell out the picture of a state sunk in a twentieth century version of the Dark Ages. In all of the forty-eight states of the nation at that time, in whatever category one might choose, Louisiana ranked close to the bottom. The state was thirty-ninth in average gross income with a figure of $1,270. It was forty-fourth in the number of farms with piped water; forty-fifth in the number of farms with electric lights; forty-seventh in the number of farms with electric motors.

The state's road and bridge system belonged back in the horse-and-buggy days of the previous century. There were no bridges connecting the great port of New Orleans with important inland areas. Even in 1928, with the age of the automobile changing the life of the nation, Louisiana had no road system worthy of the name. Estimates of the number of hard-surfaced roads vary, but an official memorandum in the files of the state highway commission shows that the entire state had only thirty-one miles of concrete roads, with twenty more under construction; only sixty-five miles of asphalt roads, with four more under construction. Almost all the roads, nearly 6,000 miles of them, were made of gravel that turned into quagmires in Louisiana's drenching, semitropical rains. It became a sick joke that the state was literally sunk "in the mud."

Even more shocking was Louisiana's record in education. The state did not even provide school books for its children; they had to purchase their own. Louisiana was next to last among the forty-eight states in literacy. Sixteen per cent of its adult population was illiterate. In rural areas, where most of the people lived, over 14 per cent of white males had not completed a single year of schooling, and four out of ten on the farms had not finished the fourth grade.

It was a dismal picture, but the state's ruling classes could not have cared less. As one member of the upper caste recalled years later: "We were secure. We were the old families. We had what we wanted. We didn't bother anybody. All we wanted was to keep it." Huey Long was determined not to let them keep it.

In this primitive state, he was a human primitive. He was earthy, boorish, supremely clever. He was determined and utterly ruthless. And these qualities made him the master of all Louisiana.

Huey Long was born August 30, 1893, on a farm outside Winnfield in Winn Parish in north-central Louisiana. In later life, he would boast that he had been born in a log cabin, and he would picture himself as a poor boy who had had to labor from dawn to dusk on a miserable farm —and who often hadn't had enough to eat. The description was phony. Huey, indeed, had been born in a log house, but it was one that had dimensions more like a mansion; certainly, it was no log cabin. Nor was the Long family ever close to destitution. Huey's father, Huey P. Long, Sr., was one of the largest landowners in the Winnfield area, and he became so prosperous that, in 1907, he built a regular southern mansion with white columns supporting porches that ran around the front and side of the house on both the first and second floors.

The Long family was poor only in the sense that they came from a farm-poor district and were several leagues removed from Louisiana's planter aristocracy. The land around Winnfield was thin and poor, not suited to raising cotton, the money crop of the South; and so Huey Sr., a clever man, concentrated on raising hogs and cattle. Though he never possessed any great amount of hard cash, he still saw to it that his children had educational advantages. In a section in which the only reading fare in most households was the local newspaper, the Long family subscribed to national magazines and built a small library. Huey's mother read to the family every day from the Bible, and the children had available to them the works of Shakespeare, Dickens, Poe, and other classical authors.

Young Huey was so bright that, by the time he was twelve, he had become known as the town pest. He was always butting in and trying to tell his elders how to run their businesses, a trait that did not endear him to those he was trying to advise. He would do anything to gain attention. When a circus came to town, he ran out into the street and pitched a stone at an elephant. When a train stopped, he would crawl under the wheels as if to examine the undercarriage, and the whole train would have to be held up until he could be dragged to safety. He would stop at nothing in his effort to draw all eyes to himself.

A show-off, he was also something of a coward. He had a sharp tongue, and he did not hesitate to use it. This, among boys, can be almost guaranteed to lead to a fist-fight, but when blows were about to be struck, Huey would walk away from the fight he had started and leave the battling to his younger and stronger brother, Earl. It was a trait that was to remain with Huey throughout his life; he was a blusterer, and he often tried to pretend that he engaged in bloody combat. But the evidence seems to be that he almost always ran instead of fighting; and when he became a political power, he was always in such fear of his life that he surrounded himself with gun-toting bodyguards, watchdogs who were to fail him in the one moment he needed them most.

Such was the boy who grew up in Winnfield and began learning about politics at an early age. Winn Parish was a radical district, especially so during Huey Long's formative years.

The 1890s were a black period for farmers. In the South and West, the depression of those years bit so deep that many farmers lost their holdings to mortgage companies and were reduced to trying to grub out a living as tenants on someone else's land. A poor district like Winn felt the pinch especially hard; and when a third party known as the People's, or the Populist, Party was founded, the voters of Winn joined the political rebellion.

The Populists (not entirely without reason) saw the federal government as being dominated by great corporations and Wall Street money, and they proposed radical reforms to curb big business and give government control over the economy. Conservatives were horrified and scared, but suffering farmers rallied in great numbers to the Populist cause. Though Huey's father never joined the Populists, he sympathized with much of their program, and there is little doubt that young Huey had bred into him at an early age a deep distrust of corporate power.

This early prejudice was reinforced by another strong streak in his character. As a young man it did not take the highly alert Huey Long—he who always had to dominate every situation, who always had to be the center of attention—very long to realize that a poor farm boy from Winn was a distinct outsider. As far as the smug, snooty powers of Louisiana were concerned, Huey Long would always be a crude, redneck hillbilly not at all in their class; and, since this was so and there was no changing it, Huey apparently decided quite early to gain power by playing up to the image the power brokers had of him. Since the poor and downtrodden were far more numerous than the power elite, Huey's log-cabin, hillbilly act placed him on the side of the great masses of the people and gave him almost automatically the basis for a huge following.

Huey Long began his career as a traveling salesman. By all the evidence, he was one of those engaging and persuasive talkers who, as the old saying goes, could sell refrigerators to the Eskimos. Wherever he went, he set sales records; but, unfortunately for him, the firms for which he worked always seemed plagued with some kind of economic disaster. When they folded, there were stretches between jobs when Huey had no work, and so he turned his eyes to the law. There were several reasons for this: his older brother, Julius, whom he had much admired as a boy, was a successful lawyer; lawyers made good money; and the law was a steppingstone to politics.

Huey Long had always intended to become a politician. He had it all worked out in that brilliant mind of his. About this brilliance there could be no question. Huey had a photographic memory. He could scan an entire page of a book and recite it word for word, a quality that enabled him to cram enough law into his head to be admitted to the bar in a year's time. A lawyer at twenty-one, he was already planning far ahead. Rose McConnell, who was to become his wife, later recalled for Professor T. Harry Williams, who has written the definitive biography of Long, that Huey Long had his future all planned out when she first met him. Though he was only a teen-aged traveling salesman at the time, he told her just how it was going to be. First, he would seek and win a secondary state office; he would use this as a political base and become governor; he would then be elected to the United States Senate— and, finally, he would become President. "It almost gave you the cold chills to hear him tell about it," Mrs. Long said.

In 1918, having established himself as a lawyer and having won some remarkable cases, Huey decided it was time for politics. But the big question was: what office should he seek?

The best version of how he came to make up his mind seems to be this: he was sitting around in a Winnfield store one day, talking politics with a bunch of cronies. Somebody suggested he run for the post of railroad commissioner. What was a railroad commissioner? Long wondered. He got out a copy of the state constitution and discovered that the commission had three members, each elected from a different district of Louisiana. The term was for six years; the salary $3,000, an adequate income in those days. Perhaps more important to Huey Long was the fact that this so-called railroad commission, though it had slumbered peacefully for years, had a lot of potential power. It set the rates charged by railroads, steamboats, sleeping cars, telephone and telegraph services—and, most important, the fees charged by oil pipelines owned by major oil companies for transporting oil. Huey Long decided that this was the post for him.

Once he entered the campaign, he threw himself into it with characteristic, whirlwind energy. He and his brother-in-law packed the back of an old Overland car with circulars and posters, and they crisscrossed the northern Louisiana district, tacking up campaign literature at every available spot. Huey, who often worked twenty hours out of twenty-four, would keep on the vote trail far into the night. He would chug up to a lonely farmhouse at some ungodly hour after everyone had gone to bed; he would rouse the farmer and his wife, and introduce himself. Instead of being outraged over sleep disturbed, most persons seemed to feel flattered; they reasoned that Huey Long must think they were important to put himself out by coming to call on them at such a late hour. The result was Long's first political victory.

All Louisiana soon became aware that the railroad commission was no longer a sleeping watchdog. Huey Long had hardly warmed his official chair before he began blasting away at Standard Oil. Independent oil producers —and Huey himself had at one time had an interest in one of these independent companies—charged that Standard refused to transport their oil through its pipeline system at the very time it was importing huge quantities of Mexican oil. Huey demanded that the governor and legislature act to protect their own Louisiana oil industry.

The instant he spoke out, lobbyists and lawyers for Standard descended upon the governor and the legislature. Since Louisiana government for decades had cowered before this kind of business might, nothing was done to help the independent oil producers. Huey Long was not unhappy; indeed, nothing could have suited him better. The business interests and politicians of the state had given him a political issue. He roared that Standard was an "octopus" and that the ruling politicians were its slaves. He made so much noise, he appealed so strongly to the common people against "the interests," that Louisianians everywhere began to talk about him and ask: "Who is this Huey Long?"

Now on the eve of his sensational political career, Huey

Long was about 5 feet 11 inches tall, weighing 160 pounds. He had the beginnings of a paunch that would soon add another fifteen pounds to his weight. His hair was reddish-brown and unruly, with one lock usually curling over his forehead; his face was round and jowly, its most distinguishing feature a fleshy nose that tipped saucily upward at the end. He had a deep-cleft, dimpled chin, and this gave him a pixyish look when he smiled.

He was always in motion. He never walked, but always moved at a pace like a half-run so that everyone had to trot to keep up with him. On the public platform, he was never still. His head would jerk, his shoulders twitch, his arms wave wildly like a windmill. All the time, he would be striding up and down, thundering his attack on "the interests." He could keep this up for two hours at a stretch under a boiling Louisiana sun, a whirling dervish of sound and movement.

When he began campaigning, he was probably the sloppiest dresser Louisiana voters had ever seen. His clothes were always rumpled. His trousers were always too short to reach his shoe tops; and, no matter what color suit he wore, he always sported white shoes and socks. It was an attire more suited to a bum than a rising politician, except for one splashy detail. After one of his early law cases, Huey Long had acquired a large diamond which he had set into a ring. This always flashed blindingly from his gesturing hands, and its sparkle was matched by that of another diamond set in his disordered shirt front. The effect was that of an uncouth country boy, a show-off who had acquired some riches but had no taste. Huey Long didn't care. If he was a country boy with diamonds, he was appealing to country boys without diamonds; and he reckoned correctly that they would like him because he seemed one of them—and that they would envy him a bit because those diamonds showed what a clever country boy like themselves might acquire.

This was the man who now kept all Louisiana in an uproar. From the vantage point of his official post on the Public Service Commission, as it was now called, Huey fired a barrage of charges alleging that practically the entire government of Louisiana had been bought. One of his principal targets was Governor John M. Parker. Huey's attacks on the big oil companies, which were not paying the state a dime for the oil extracted from Louisiana soil, had touched such a sensitive nerve that the governor felt compelled to call in representatives of Standard Oil and other big producers. In effect, he said to them: "Really, boys, you should be paying some taxes, you know." He pointed out that the oil companies were reaping "a golden harvest" from the state and that they really had an obligation to help the state from which they drew such wealth. The plea seemed reasonable, but the answer of the oil men shocked the governor. They told him in effect that they didn't give a hoot what happened to Louisiana and its people; they just didn't intend to be taxed.

The public storm that Huey Long had raised, however, wouldn't go away. Governor Parker just had to get some kind of a tax—even if it was just a token tax. The oil men finally recognized that the politicians were going to have to cave in to popular demand, and so they and the governor reached what was afterwards called "a gentlemen's agreement." The oil firms agreed to pay a 2 per cent severance tax on the oil taken from Louisiana wells, but they were still fearful and suspicious. Who, they wanted to know, was going to write the tax bill? "You gentlemen can write it," Parker said. The oil lobbyists almost fell on their faces in surprise, but naturally they grabbed up the governor's offer.

This private deal between the governor and the oil industry was a made-to-order issue for Huey Long. When the legislature assembled, every member found upon his desk a circular prepared by Huey. It charged flatly that Standard Oil now controlled the state. As proof, it cited Parker's private agreement with Standard Oil, and it asked whether the legislators were such "fallen chattels" that they would sit still and let the state's tax laws be written by Standard attorneys at 26 Broadway, New York City.

Huey followed up this first blast with two other circulars. These charged that his two fellow Public Service Commissioners were also pawns of big-business interests. The Cumberland Telegraph and Telephone Company was seeking to raise its rates, and Huey implied that his two fellow commissioners had reneged on a promise to oppose the increase because they had been bought. He added that he could have benefited handsomely himself if he had been willing to accept a bribe.

These sensational charges shattered the beehive of Louisiana officialdom, and outraged officials, angrily swarming, sought some way to get Huey Long. The legislature considered impeaching him, but that meant his charges would have to be investigated. And who knew where *that* might lead? Governor Parker finally resolved the difficulty by having Huey arrested for criminal libel. The trial was a fiasco. The governor admitted he had let Standard Oil attorneys write the tax law. Huey, in his own defense, cited this admission by the governor and argued that he had not attacked Parker personally but had questioned his administration, his handling of state affairs. The judge hearing the case tried to come up with a verdict that would please both sides. He found Huey guilty, then fined him $1, sentenced him to thirty days in jail—and suspended the sentence. Huey hailed the meaningless verdict as a victory.

His name was now becoming a byword in the state, and for the next two years he kept it constantly in the headlines. He kept hounding Standard Oil. He kept harping on the telephone-rate case that meant higher tariffs for 66,000 Louisiana telephone owners. And he found a new issue in a bridge-building controversy in New Orleans. A private corporation sought state approval for a toll bridge connecting the city to the mainland. Huey trumpeted that this would give insiders a bridge monopoly—and the privilege of gouging the riding public to the end of time. All of these varied issues made Huey Long unique, a Louisiana political leader who deliberately opposed the powerful and sought the support of the great mass of common people.

It was something that had never happened in all of Louisiana's past history. As one Long leader later said, "You had either to be endorsed by the sugar barons, the banks, or the railroads. . . . The idea of you running in this state without them being your boss was unheard of." Yet this was what Huey Long did.

In 1923 he made his first bid for the governorship. He was beaten. Conservative interests and their mouthpieces in the press shouted that he was politically dead. They rejoiced too soon. He had been defeated because he had hardly any support in New Orleans; but even with the powerful New Orleans machine against him, he had run a formidable race. And he had done it, obviously, only because the poor people of Louisiana were beginning to stir and follow their champion.

Four years later Long challenged the state's power brokers again. He had learned from the 1923 campaign that he had two simple and powerful issues working for him. His call for free textbooks and for the hard-topping of virtually all state roads had been immensely popular. Incredibly, the state's conservative forces had not budged on even such simple and obvious issues. They were content to leave the road system sunk in the mud; they saw free textbooks as a sign of creeping communism; they fought municipal ownership of utilities; they opposed even the regulation of utilities; they were against free bridges into New Orleans; they wouldn't even back legislation making cheap natural gas, so abundant in Louisiana oil fields, available to the public. In effect, they abandoned every issue to Huey Long.

And Huey, the supreme politician, took full advantage of every opportunity they gave him. Banners above the platforms on which he spoke always carried this slogan: "Every Man a King, But No One Wears a Crown." He sometimes acted like a boor to show that he was still just a country boy at heart. Never to be forgotten was the occasion on which a wealthy family gave a luncheon in his honor. T. Harry Williams, in his prize-winning biography, *Huey Long*, describes it this way: "The dining room sparkled with china and silver. Huey came in, glanced around contemptuously, and swept his place setting to the floor. 'Give me a knife and fork,' he bellowed. 'I don't know how to handle all this cutlery.' "

When his leading opponent, Congressman Riley J. Wilson, tried the common touch by proclaiming he had gone barefoot as a boy, Huey went him one better with a witty sally that convulsed his audience. "I was born barefoot," he said. He mocked his foes with the kind of savage wit that sent them into fuming rage. He labeled an opponent, a pompous man with a large dark mustache, "Colonel Bow Wow." And he attacked Mayor Lee E. Thomas, of Shreveport, who was backing one of his opponents, so repeatedly and so scathingly that Thomas finally could not stand it and sought recourse in legal action.

Thomas had spent a lifetime in politics, holding one office after another, and Huey implied he was worse than a hog. "You take a pig, even the hog is ashamed of himself and weans himself when he gets to be a good-sized shoat," Huey said. "But you take a pie eater and trough feeder like L. E. Thomas who has been sucking the pap for thirty-five years. You cannot wean him at all." On another occasion, he told this fanciful and devastating story about Thomas: a Chinaman, a Fiji Islander, and Thomas made a bet about who could stay longest in a room with a pole-cat. The Chinaman lasted ten minutes; the Fiji Islander, fifteen. Then it was Thomas' turn. "He went in and stayed five minutes, and the polecat ran out," Huey said. Thomas was so enraged he sued Huey for slander, but the suit was dismissed on a technicality.

Louisiana had never seen a political campaign like it. This was, of course, the Democratic primary, for in those days Louisiana was a one-party state and whoever won the Democratic nomination was certain of election. When the votes were counted, Huey Long had 126,842 to 81,747 for Wilson, his nearest rival. He did not have a majority of the votes, however, and this meant that a runoff election should be held. But Huey Long's lead was so huge his opposition collapsed, and he became governor.

The powerful conservative forces of Louisiana still did not understand the man with whom they had to deal. The South has had more than its share of ranting demagogues. Many have campaigned on racial bigotry, the "nigger" issue, but Long rarely did. Others have posed as champions of the people. But almost all, once elected, have made their compromises and become the tools of the interests they had seemed to fight. Huey Long was different. He meant what he said, and he had a dictatorial streak in him that would brook no opposition.

He set out almost immediately to make the entire government—the legislature, the state commissions, the courts—his captive. He wangled control of both houses of the legislature with job promises. He stacked every board and commission with his own appointees. If the commissioners already holding office had been appointed for fixed terms, he got the legislature to change the terms so he could fire them and name his own men. These new men were not free agents. Huey demanded they sign blank resignations before he appointed them. This meant that, the instant they refused to do his bidding, he had only to type in a date on their resignations and they were out.

His legislative program followed his campaign promises. New Orleans consumers were paying exceptionally high rates for manufactured gas; Huey drafted a bill to bring Louisiana's cheap and plentiful natural gas to the city. Other legislation provided for free textbooks and a bond issue to hasten highway construction. The conservatives, bent on their own doom, fought every measure. "They opposed everything he was for," one of them said later.

In so acting, they made themselves perfect targets for Huey Long's steamroller. The new governor drove his program through the legislature with lightning speed. The rules called for legislation to be referred to an appropriate committee after it was introduced. There it would be considered; perhaps hearings would be held; and the bill would be given three readings on the floor before the vote on final passage was taken. Huey Long ordered the rules suspended; his bills had to be passed unchanged in a single day. When an important measure was up for a vote, he would storm into the legislature himself, stride up and down the aisles, and bark out his commands: vote aye or nay, as the case might be. If a legislator happened to be absent, Huey would cast his vote for him. No governor, of course, had any right to do this, but Huey Long did it. He had to be the center of the action, just as he had been as a boy. "I can't stay out," he said. "I just got to be there."

It was at this time, in the early days of his administration, that he acquired the nickname of "the Kingfish." A large part of the nation listened at that time to the "Amos 'n' Andy" radio show. The program was popular with Long and his followers. One of the characters in the show was named the Kingfish, and Huey became fascinated with the title. Soon he was applying it to himself. When he telephoned someone, he would say simply, "This is the Kingfish"—and no one in Louisiana could possibly doubt who was talking.

The conservatives became so infuriated that they organized a band of legislators known as "the Dynamite Squad." They opposed anything Huey Long was for. And they set out to get the governor.

The first real test came on Long's bill to tax the big oil companies. Standard Oil, by all accounts, rallied the opposition. A Standard lobbyist hired an entire floor of rooms in one of the best hotels in the state capital in Baton Rouge. There he held open court for members of the legislature. Money flowed like water spilling over a dam. Huey Long in radio speeches charged that Standard was buying up the legislature, and he was not far wrong. Some of the legislators themselves later looked back on those days with a kind of sad longing. "You could pick up $15,000 or $20,000 any evening then," one of them later said.

The result was Long's first defeat. The legislature refused to pass his oil tax measure.

Following up this victory, the conservatives began a drive to impeach Long and remove him from office. They filed a long series of charges. The most serious accused him of waging a private vendetta against Standard Oil; of misusing his powers with the blank-resignation system; of promising legislators well-paying jobs for voting his way— a practice by no means unusual in politics, but one that had a certain odor of bribery about it.

In seeking to rally opposition to Long, however, the conservatives could not help exposing themselves. They were blind where their own self-interests were concerned. At one mass meeting, they actually passed a resolution condemning any measures that sought "to impose tax burdens upon industries" in Louisiana. In other words, the average man could be taxed on his farm or home, but big businesses wouldn't be taxed at all on the fortunes they were making in Louisiana. Here was a grand program to set before the people.

But the conservatives, concerned only with their own pocketbooks and privileges, could see nothing wrong with it. They pressed their attack and got the lower house of the legislature to vote impeachment. The case then went to the Senate, where a two-thirds vote was needed to remove Long from office.

Once more the money flowed. A huge fund was raised and funneled through political fixers in an effort to buy enough votes to oust Long. Agents of the corrupt New Orleans political machine, large rolls of bills in their hands, were seen roaming the corridors of the state house, trying to "persuade" legislators. In one case $40,000 was offered for a vote; in another, a Long senator was offered $25,000, and when he refused that, the offer was raised to $50,000. This senator spurned the offer and told the man who made it he would kick him out of the house if he called again.

Huey Long did not have this kind of money to offer, but he did have state patronage—and that meant the kind of contracts and jobs that were worth fortunes. He didn't hesitate to use everything he had, and so there were times when the Long forces and the anti-Long forces came into collision as each tried to buy the vote of some wavering senator. Finally, after all the tugging and hauling, Huey Long wrapped up enough votes to defeat the impeachers. He needed fourteen votes in the Senate, and he got fifteen. These supporters signed what became known as "the Round Robin," pledging themselves to stand with Huey to the end; and, with this document in his pocket, Long was safe.

This life-and-death political struggle, however, had left its mark upon him. He was forever grateful to the signers of the Round Robin, and he rewarded them throughout the rest of his career with whatever they asked for that was in his power to give. And he was as vengeful toward his foes as he was grateful to his friends. He set out to destroy those who had tried to destroy him, and this meant the whole complex of powerful, conservative, big-business forces that had been behind the votes cast in the Senate against him. If he had had dictatorial tendencies before— and he had had—he was now determined to become the complete dictator, to determine policy on every public issue and to destroy utterly the whole power complex of Louisiana.

Though impeachment had been defeated, conservative forces still controlled the legislature and were in a position to balk Huey Long's ever-growing programs. The Great Depression of the 1930s had now settled over the land like some horrible blight; men were out of work, families were starving, banks were failing, business was at a standstill. Only Huey Long saw in this national disaster the seeds of opportunity. Now, he declared, was the time to build. Now was the time to bring Louisiana into the twentieth century. More roads should be surfaced; bridges should be thrown across the Mississippi to New Orleans; a new state capitol built. Not only could these huge construction projects be completed at rock-bottom depression prices, but they would provide jobs and stimulate the economy of all Louisiana. Die-hard conservatives were, of course, hor-rified at the prospect of spending millions upon millions of dollars on such huge public works, and Long's program was stalled in the legislature.

Balked by the old guard, Long decided to take his case once more to the people. U.S. Senator Joseph E. Ransdell was up for re-election in 1930, and Huey Long, though he still had two years to serve in the governor's office, decided to oppose him. He would make the senatorial election, he proclaimed, a referendum on his programs for Louisiana. Conservatives were shocked to the bottom of their sensitive souls at the idea of hillbilly Huey Long running against Ransdell, "a gentleman" of the old school. Newspaper editorialists and orators frothed with rage. They denounced Huey Long as "a freak," a man of "malformed and diseased mind," an "ultra-Socialist" who was more radical than either Marx or Lenin, "a degenerate in mind and morals," a man who made the famous bandit Jesse James look "like a gentleman." One political boss summed it all up, roaring: "Long has the face of a clown, the heart of a petty larceny burglar, and the disposition of a tyrant."

The Kingfish met all this with simple, biting ridicule. When Ransdell began his campaign, a group of women admirers presented him with a feather duster. This was supposed to symbolize the purity of his record, and Ransdell, with a bit of foolish oratory, accepted the feather duster as if it had been the Congressional Medal of Honor. Huey Long hopped upon the performance with cries of glee. Thereafter, throughout the campaign, he went up and down the state, hardly ever mentioning Ransdell's name, but proclaiming he was running against "Old Feather Duster."

The issues and the wit were all on the side of Huey Long, and he swamped Ransdell by a vote of 149,640 to 111,451. He almost carried New Orleans, the stronghold of opposition, losing the city to Ransdell by a mere 4,000 votes. At 37 Huey Long now wore two official hats. He was the governor of Louisiana, and he was the U.S. senator from Louisiana. And even the die-hards of the old order collapsed and decided they would have to make peace with him.

Such a truce could only be temporary, for each side hated and distrusted the other. But, while it lasted, Huey Long's improvement programs whipped through the legislature. The road and bridge network was extended, the new capitol built. Educational, medical, and health services were upgraded. Huey Long practically took over Louisiana State University, poured millions of dollars into it, and set up a new medical school there to rival the established school at Tulane. All of this was on the positive side, but there were other, negative and ugly features to Long's rule.

Huey Long was a dictator at heart. He had seized power and he would keep it—and he didn't care what means he used. All state employees had to kick back 10 per cent of their wages for weeks at election time to build his political campaign fund. He controlled the election machinery with an iron hand, striking off the voting registers the names of foes and padding the final ballot box count so that his candidates sometimes received more votes in a given district than there were voters. He surrounded himself with a gun-toting bodyguard; and, whenever his rule was threatened, he called out the state police and the national guard to intimidate his opponents. In time, Louisiana became an armed camp, with Long and anti-Long forces facing each other, fingers itching on the triggers of shotguns, rifles, and revolvers.

The tension and the hate increased with each passing year, and Huey Long in his person was one reason that it did. He was a drunk—and a nasty drunk. He had begun drinking in his traveling salesman's days, and he had kept at it through the years. But he could not carry his liquor well. A few drinks would set him off, and then he was

almost uncontrollable. He was often deliberately coarse
and boorish. He took a vicious delight in offending the
cultured and pompous. When the captain of a visiting
German cruiser and the German consul in New Orleans
made a formal call upon him, he received them in his hotel
room in rumpled pajamas. The proper Germans were insulted, and the affair became an international incident.
When a newspaper reporter took offense at being called
an unprintable name and swung at Long, hitting a glanc-
ing blow, the governor's ever-present bodyguards seized
and held the offender while Huey, ever a bully, struck the
helpless man in the face, thus satisfying his honor.

Any other man, having been elected to the U.S. Senate,
would have gone to Washington, taken his seat, and left
Louisiana to a successor. But not Huey Long. He had
fallen out with his lieutenant governor, Paul N. Cyr, and
he was determined that Cyr should not get his hands on
the reins of government. Therefore, he stayed on in Louisiana, waiting until he could put in the governor's chair a
man whom he could control. The one he selected for this
honor was Oscar K. Allen, a longtime supporter from
Winn Parish. In the election of 1931, Allen swept the
state, with whole election districts under Long control giving him thousands of votes to not one for his opponent.

Even with Allen's election, Huey Long would not leave
Louisiana. Allen could not take office until May, 1932,
and Long was determined not to let Cyr become governor
for a day or a minute. Cyr was so infuriated he tried a
force-play. He proclaimed himself governor, arguing that
since Huey's election as senator had been certified to
Washington he could no longer act as governor. Huey
responded by calling out the state police and ringing the

governor's mansion and state capitol in Baton Rouge with machine guns to keep Cyr out.

Safe behind this army, Huey Long next made one of those lightning moves that were so slick they left everyone dumbfounded. Since Cyr had proclaimed himself governor, Huey said, he could no longer be lieutenant governor; he had left the post, and it was vacant. Therefore, Huey swore in as lieutenant governor Alvin O. King, president of the Senate and a safe Long man. With King backstopping him, Huey then left quietly for Washington, took his oath of office as senator, and had King sworn in as governor in Baton Rouge. Cyr was outflanked, made to look ridiculous and—such was Huey's power—was even ousted from the Baton Rouge hotel in which he had set up headquarters.

It was farce on a colossal scale, and it made Louisiana the laughing stock of the nation. All across the country, pranksters got into the act, having themselves solemnly inducted in dummy ceremonies as "governor" of Louisiana. The game even extended to the "swearing in" of legions of "lieutenant governors," much to the amusement of the Kingfish and the frustration and rage of his enemies.

In Washington, Huey Long burst upon the national scene like some uncontrollable force of nature. He was the radical battering at the doors of tradition, denouncing the wealthy and the powerful. The nation was now sunk in the deepest pit of depression. Banks were failing in increasing numbers, millions of men (one quarter of all adult males in the nation) were out of work, farmers were being driven off their lands by mortgage companies, and there seemed no end to the worsening disaster. The trouble was, Long quickly proclaimed, that the wealth of the country was in the hands of a tiny few. It had to be redistributed.

Otherwise, he said boldly, there would be revolution—
communism. When he was denounced for this "soak the
rich" policy, he cried: "It is no campaign to soak the rich.
It is a campaign to save the rich. It is a campaign the
success of which they will wish for when it is too late."

He hammered at the theme in speech after speech. He
charged that 540 men on Wall Street made at least one
million dollars each a year—a combined income more
than that of all the farmers in the nation. He introduced a
resolution providing that no one should be permitted to
have an income of more than one million dollars a year
and that no person should be allowed to inherit more than
five million dollars in his lifetime. Democrats and Republicans both were shocked. Here, indeed, was a wild radical
loose and rampaging in the U. S. Senate.

Huey Long didn't care what anyone thought. He defied
even the leaders of his own party. The Majority Leader in
the Senate was Joseph T. Robinson, an Arkansas Democrat. Huey vowed that Robinson was no better than a
Hoover Republican. In May, 1932, after having jabbed at
Robinson on several previous occasions, he attacked the
Arkansan directly. Robinson's law firm, he said, represented forty-three corporations, including some of the nation's largest oil, utility, and chain-store companies. He
would not, he said, follow the lead of a man who was a
corporation attorney.

Old-time senators were shocked. One firm rule of the
Senate is that senators must be polite to each other, that
they must not cast slurs or call names. When a senator
objected that Huey was violating this sacred rule, the Kingfish was compelled to sit down for a minute, but he could
not be silenced for long. Jumping to his feet, he said with
reverse English:

"I want now to disclaim that I have the slightest motive of saying, or that in my heart I believe, that such a man could be influenced in any vote which he casts in this body by the fact that that association might mean hundreds of thousands of millions of dollars in the way of lucrative fees."

Even the Senate had to laugh.

Huey Long was now a force to be reckoned with, not just in Louisiana but in the nation. In the campaign of 1932, he loomed large on the American scene. The junior senator from Arkansas was a quiet little woman, Mrs. Hattie Caraway. Her husband, Thaddeus, had been senator, but he had died in office. The politicians of Arkansas had decided to let the widow serve out the remaining year of the term, but they had no intention of letting her be reelected. Huey Long had discovered, however, that Hattie Caraway voted for the common people on economic issues, and he decided that *he* would save her Senate seat for her. Invading neighboring Arkansas with a caravan of sound trucks, he put on a whirlwind, seven-day campaign. Huge crowds turned out to hear him. "We're all here to pull a lot of pot-bellied politicians off a little woman's neck," Huey told them. Then he went on to describe the condition of the nation, starvation in the midst of plenty. He denounced the system that permitted such obvious wrongs, and soon he had the Arkansas crowds whooping. A politician who witnessed Huey's first performance after he crossed the border wired friends in Little Rock: "A cyclone just went through here and is headed your way. Very few trees left standing and even these are badly scarred up."

Arkansas had never seen such a performance. In just seven days, Huey Long turned the Senate contest upside down, and Mrs. Caraway, who had been given no chance, won in a landslide.

Swinging back into Louisiana, Huey went after the second Senate seat in his home state. It was held by Edwin Broussard, whom Huey called "one of Wall Street's own." Huey put one of his own veteran, faithful followers, John H. Overton, into the race against Broussard; and, once more, the Long machine steamrollered all opposition.

Having settled matters in Arkansas and Louisiana, the Kingfish now turned to the national scene. He had supported New York Governor Franklin D. Roosevelt for the Democratic Presidential nomination, and he was eager to campaign for Roosevelt. But Roosevelt's supporters were not enthusiastic. They distrusted the flashy, wild-swinging, boorish Kingfish; they looked upon him as something of a clown. And so they sent him to the western corn-belt states where, they reasoned, he couldn't do much harm. Huey took the assignment and swept through the Dakotas, Nebraska, and Kansas with the same cyclonic force Arkansas had known. Before he was finished, five state chairmen in the region wired James A. Farley, Roosevelt's campaign manager: "If you have any doubtful state, send Huey Long into it."

When Roosevelt was elected, Long expected to influence him. He had pressed his redistribution of wealth ideas on Roosevelt, and he apparently thought that Roosevelt had agreed. Huey Long had also underrated Roosevelt. He thought at first that the smooth-mannered Hyde Park gentleman lacked strength and was someone he could dominate. He was, of course, wrong. Huey Long, who always had to be first, had met another man who always had to be first—and this man was now the President.

The life-plan that Huey Long had outlined to his young

bride years before—the step-by-step rise from a minor state office of governor, to U.S. senator, then to President —had been followed perfectly up to this point. Only the final leap remained. But in the way now stood a man as clever and as tough as Long himself. The Kingfish began to realize this. Returning from one interview with Roosevelt, he told a friend: "I found a man as smart as I am. I don't know if I can travel with him."

It was not long before the split between the two was in the open. Huey Long began to denounce Roosevelt as too conservative. Roosevelt's policies, he said, would not cure depression ills. Huey alone had the saving formula. And on February 23, 1934, he announced it to the American public.

Speaking over a nationwide radio hookup, he announced the formation of the Share Our Wealth Society. Its motto: Every Man a King. His program, as he described it, sent cold shudders up and down the spines of all the wealthy and powerful classes in the nation.

The federal government would impose a capital-levy tax that would prevent any one family from owning a fortune of more than five million dollars. The income tax rates would be raised to prevent anyone from earning more than one million dollars a year. Revenue from these taxes would guarantee every family a "homestead" worth $5,000. The government would guarantee every family a basic income of from $2,000 to $3,000. There would be other benefits. The aged would be given pensions of $30 a month; all qualified students would be guaranteed free college education; veterans would be paid liberal bonuses; and the government would regulate employment, limiting the work week to thirty hours and granting workers a month's vacation each year, steps that should force the hiring of more men.

There were obvious flaws in the plan. Just how great fortunes, consisting of huge stock holdings or vast tracts of land, could be carved up and "distributed," Huey didn't say. Obviously, the ownership of practically all of the nation's great industries would be affected, but who would then control, who would organize and run them? The Kingfish didn't explain. To the powers that ran the country, it seemed he was spouting the wildest, most irresponsible radicalism, but it is obvious, looking back, that some of his ideas weren't so wild. In less than two years, Social Security would come into being, providing old-age pensions; in less than six, the government would legislate a forty-hour work week, which would be reduced still further for many as the years passed; and in the 1970s a guaranteed family income plan of some kind seems almost certain of adoption to replace the welfare system.

But in 1934 none of this was obvious. Huey Long was looked upon as a menace, and a most dangerous one, for he stirred the grass roots. His Share Our Wealth plan swept the South and rural districts like a prairie fire. His senatorial office was deluged with sacks of mail. In one week 140,000 letters poured in. Share Our Wealth clubs sprang up in every state. By 1935 they claimed a membership of 4,684,000, and they seemed to be growing.

In shock, the power brokers set out to bring down Huey Long. Roosevelt, considering him a fascist, threw the full weight of his administration against the Long machine. Federal patronage and federal works projects in Louisiana were placed in the hands of Long's enemies. The Senate began an investigation of Overton's election amid loud

cries of fraud. Long's foes tried to get both him and Overton kicked out of the Senate. One complaint, seriously
investigated by a Senate committee, even alleged that
Huey was a madman who should be confined to an insane
asylum instead of being allowed to run loose in Senate
corridors.

In Louisiana itself, elections became increasingly exer-
cises in pure terror. Armed bands faced each other; mar-
tial law was decreed. The Baton Rouge district had long
been the section of the state most hostile to the Kingfish.
When a congressman from the area died, Huey tried to
call a quickie election, with the only name on the ballot
that of his hand-picked candidate. His political foes re-
acted in outrage. "Shotgun clubs" were formed, and
armed men burst into courthouses, seized the ballots and
set fire to them. When the Long machine tried to truck in
new ballots under state police escort, the "shotgun" squads
riddled the trucks with pellets and forced them to turn
back. Hodding Carter, a newspaper publisher and fierce
anti-Longite, later described how he lay in the dark night,
shotgun in hand, revolver at his side, ready to battle the
national guard if Long sent it in. Long didn't, and the next
day Carter was one of a roving, armed patrol that visited
all the voting booths to make certain they stayed empty.

This was only one of many such clashes as hate swept
Louisiana. It was a blind, fierce, unreasoning hate. As
even Hodding Carter was later to admit, the anti-Long
forces had no program; they simply opposed, sometimes
with shotguns, everything that Long advocated.

The result was that, in a state in which there were no
angels, Huey Long held his grip on the great mass of
common people. He was the only politician who had ever

done anything for them. He had given them good roads, bridges, free textbooks, better education, better medical care. And he held out to them the dream of a utopia in which Louisiana would become the testing ground for his Share Our Wealth program.

Carried away by his own vision of a glorious future, he became increasingly dictatorial. Here was a man who had the wit, the brilliance, the oratorical gifts of a great political leader; he could have ruled, it would seem, through the democratic process. But the fierceness and violence of his opposition, acting on a nature that could not stand the smallest check, drove him to extremes—drove him to seek a tyrant's vengeance on all who opposed him.

With a legislature brought to heel, he drafted legislation; he alone testified about it; he alone directed the floor fights in the lower house and the state senate, frequently dashing from one chamber to the other; he alone decided, acted, ruled. Between August, 1934, and September, 1935, he rammed 226 bills through the legislature. In one incredible session, 44 bills were enacted into law in just five days.

The effect of these laws was to place all power in the hands of Long and his puppet governor. They alone could appoint voting commissioners, guard the polls, and have custody of the ballot boxes. The national guard could be called out at any time at the whim of the governor. The state police, as Carter wrote, were swelled "into a swarm of private agents," with virtually Gestapo powers. The Long state machine could replace any district attorney it did not like. It could fire any teacher in any school district anywhere. Its State Tax Commission could change any assessment in any town or parish, rewarding friends and taxing foes out of existence. Even the appointment of local police and fire chiefs had to be approved by a Long-dominated Civil Service Commission. And one fantastic measure let the governor remove the entire city administration of Alexandria, a town in which Huey had been barraged with rotten eggs.

Democracy no longer existed in Louisiana. Even moderates became convinced that Huey Long had become power mad, and his long-time, archconservative foes were driven practically up the wall. More and more "shotgun" squads were organized, and there was increasing talk of assassination. Huey himself became convinced that he would be killed, and he surrounded himself with ever more bodyguards. They kept watch outside his door in Washington while he slept; they sat and watched in the Senate galleries when he spoke on the floor; they accompanied him, armed with revolvers and ill-concealed shotguns, whenever he went to a country club to play golf. But not even their overpowering presence, not even their protection, could save him.

On Sunday, September 8, 1935, Huey Long went to Baton Rouge, where he attended a night session of the newly assembled legislature. About 9:20 P.M. he went to the governor's office in the capitol, and he was standing in the corridor outside the door, surrounded by his guards and followers, when a thin man in a white suit stepped from behind a pillar, brushed through the ring around Huey, drew a pistol, and fired.

"I'm shot," Huey cried, clutching his stomach and staggering away down the hall.

His guards turned savagely on the assassin, gunning him down and riddling his body with sixty-one shots. The assassin was Dr. Carl Austin Weiss, a brilliant young ear, nose, and throat specialist; the son of a prominent Baton Rouge doctor; the son-in-law of a judge who was one of Huey's bitterest political enemies. Young Carl Weiss was an idealistic man who had been stirred to fury, who had been known to weep, over Huey Long's tyrannical rule, over the lost democracy of Louisiana. Long forces later charged that he was the chosen instrument of a group of plotters representing the old hide-bound conservative elements that were determined to get rid of Huey at any cost. And though there was never to be any proof, there were indeed some indications that this might have been so.

As for Huey, Carl Weiss' .32 caliber bullet had perforated his stomach, passing completely through his body. The stricken Kingfish was taken to a nearby hospital, where an emergency operation was performed. It seemed at first that he would recover, but it soon became apparent that the operating surgeon had not been thorough enough —that he had missed damage to one kidney. Huey Long was bleeding internally, and he was too weak to stand a second operation. For thirty hours, he drifted in and out of comas until, at 4:06 A.M., September 10, he died. According to those around his bedside, his last words were: "God, don't let me die. I have so much to do."

Even in death, he seemed to have a vision of those legions of the poor who were waiting for him to help them. He had been the only Southern politician of his time who had followed a dream, who had tried to help, who had not sold out. But he had become possessed by power; he had been ruled by the conviction that any means to attain his ends was justified—and so he had become a dictator. And those who realized that he had aimed at the Presidency and its enormous powers could only shudder at the thought of what might have happened had he ever fulfilled his final ambition; had he ever tried to extend to all America the kind of dictatorial rule he had imposed on Louisiana.

6

FATHER COUGHLIN

The years of the Great Depression were a breeding time for demagogues. The whole world seemed to be falling apart about the heads of its unhappy inhabitants, and the worried, the jobless, the starving wanted words of explanation—and of hope. How had it happened? What was to be done?

It was a time when millions of Americans would fall in love with Huey Long and his Share Our Wealth plan. It was a time when many millions more would hang on every word of a priest named Father Coughlin. His followers became convinced that he knew all the causes of their troubles and had all the answers. His scapegoats became their scapegoats; and, in the end, they would follow him, many of them, into the dark caverns of racial hate.

Charles E. Coughlin was an almost unknown Catholic priest until the Sunday afternoon of October 30, 1930. He had been born in Canada of Irish-American parents, and since 1926 he had been the pastor of a tiny parish in Royal Oak, Michigan, a suburb twelve miles north of Detroit. A big man weighing some two hundred pounds, he was gray-haired, blue-eyed, and immensely likable. Even those who were prepared to distrust him often fell under the spell of his Irish charm and good humor. Above all things he possessed a voice. A marvelous voice. It was

mellow, rich, manly, and heart-warming. Over the radio—
and Americans then were as wedded to the radio as later
generations were to be to television—this voice flooded
the living rooms of the nation, speaking with such charm
and intimacy that listeners felt instantly as if they knew the
speaker and could trust him. His truth became their truth.

Father Coughlin had been using this great, persuasive
voice over the radio for four years before that dramatic
Sunday afternoon in 1930. He had had a hard time building up his flock in Royal Oak. There was much prejudice
against Catholics at the time, and the Ku Klux Klan on
one occasion had burned a cross on Father Coughlin's
lawn. In 1926 a friend had introduced him to the manager
of radio station WJR in Detroit, and arrangements had
been made for Sunday afternoon broadcasts directly from
Father Coughlin's Shrine of the Little Flower. This first
series of radio talks was entitled the "Golden Hour of the
Little Flower," and it was aimed at children. It did not
deal with topics of the day except for rare, offhand re-
marks.

By the fall of 1930, however, the nation was in the grip
of the worst panic in its history. A year before, the stock
market had collapsed with a roar that had touched off an
avalanche of disaster. There had been stock market
crashes before, but none like this. Business did not revive;
it got worse. The entire nation seemed to be sickening
unto death.

The value of stocks in the nation's greatest corporations
dropped some $23 billion on the stock exchange. The
profits of 200 leading industrial concerns were off 45.9
per cent. Steel production was down 40 per cent; automobile production, off 60 per cent. Some six million men

were jobless, and even those who still had work were taking pay cut after pay cut. Farmers who had been strug-
gling the year before when wheat sold at $1.35 a bushel
now were going bankrupt with wheat selling at 76 cents a
bushel. As the disaster widened, banks failed at an alarming and ever-increasing rate. The first ten months of 1930
saw banks folding at a rate of sixty to eighty a month, and
soon it was to get worse—236 bank failures in November;
328 in December. In some towns and cities every bank
had failed, and money had gone almost out of circulation.
This was America, the greatest, richest nation on earth,
stricken with a deadly disease whose cause no man seemed
to know, whose cure seemed beyond human skill.

It was in this atmosphere of hard times and despair that
Father Coughlin launched his first free-swinging attack
upon the "money changers." The great international
bankers, men to whom money meant more than human
lives, had brought on the disaster in his view; and, unless
their evil grip was pried from the helm of the ship of
state, there would be revolution and the Communists
would take over. Father Coughlin had warned before of
the dangers of communism, but now he called upon the
"money changers" and the industrialists of the nation to
mend their ways, to see that laboring men received decent
salaries, to sacrifice profits for human welfare. If they did
not, he warned, heads almost certainly would roll.

The response was electric. The common people, who
were suffering as they had never suffered before, wanted
to know what was causing their misery, and here was this
marvelous, persuasive voice telling them that the multimil-
lionaires of Wall Street had sacrificed them on the altar of
corporate greed and stock-market shenanigans. A flood of

mail descended upon the Shrine of the Little Flower. The burden of this cascade of letters was praise for Father Coughlin and the plea: tell us more. The radio priest had hit a sensitive nerve; he had acquired, overnight, a following of millions; and the children's hour was no more.

Broadcast followed broadcast, each angrier than the one that had gone before. Father Coughlin organized the Radio League of the Little Flower, and for just one dollar, one could become a member of his holy radio crusade. Amazingly, the dollars poured down upon the head of the radio priest in a green-golden deluge. And as the dollars came in, the rich, bewitching voice became ever more excited, finding ever new and more dangerous dragons to slay. Within three months after his opening blast at the "money changers," Father Coughlin was getting 50,000 letters a week, and this was only a foretaste of things to come.

So far, he had encountered little opposition. He had attacked Communists, always a safe target. He had attacked Prohibition in a nation that detested Prohibition. And he had frothed at the "money changers" in a nation that, in its wretchedness, was prepared to blame all its ills on those who had wealth and power.

But in January, 1931, Father Coughlin suffered his first check; and, ironically, it made him a bigger hero than ever to his followers.

The Treaty of Versailles that had ended World War I had imposed back-breaking financial penalties on Germany. Some critics of the treaty contended that this was the cause of the depression. The German economy had been wrecked; international trade had been crippled; and the disaster, in this view, spread outward in ever-widening circles. Doubtless, the Treaty of Versailles was a horror (it was to be one of the causes for the rise of Hitler), but it was idiotic to blame the American depression on this cause alone. It was, however, one of the major flaws in Father Coughlin that he always oversimplified. He reduced the most complex problems to one narrow, simple issue his listeners could understand. Where there were many causes and many villains, he gave his public a single devil it could recognize and hate. And so he prepared a blast at the international bankers who, he said, had risked world peace and prosperity to save their investments in Europe.

Father Coughlin's broadcasts at this time were being carried over the Columbia Broadcasting System network. CBS already had been getting some protests from the wealthy whom Father Coughlin had attacked; and when it learned in advance about his Versailles-international bankers speech, it became worried. It put pressure on Father Coughlin to tone down his speech. The radio priest seemed to agree, saying he would talk on an entirely different subject. He did. He devoted his entire radio speech of January 4, 1931, to an account of the manner in which, he said, CBS had tried to muzzle him.

The response was incredible. Some 1,250,000 letters poured into the Shrine of the Little Flower. In all the history of radio, there had never been a deluge like it. It was little wonder that Father Coughlin became convinced he was marching at the head of a virtual army; that he represented in his person the power of the people of the nation. And so, on the following Sunday, he delivered his postponed attack on the Treaty of Versailles and the international bankers, defying CBS. The network's response was predictable. It reorganized its Sunday schedules in such a fashion that there was just no time available for Father Coughlin's broadcast.

What happened next was not so predictable. Father Coughlin organized his own radio network, buying time on twenty-six stations from Maine to Colorado at a cost of $14,000 a week. The expense was met—and more than met—by the contributions contained in the Niagara of mail that continued to descend upon his office.

Now in command of his own network, Father Coughlin knew no restraint, and his attacks ranged far and wide. In speech after speech, he denounced President Herbert Hoover, who was presiding helplessly over the deepening disaster. Father Coughlin ridiculed Hoover's Administration for "preaching to us that prosperity was just around the corner." Things were getting worse, not better, the radio priest said, and he blamed Hoover and the bankers whose "gambling and gold seeking" represented "a torture more refined" than any practiced by Roman emperors or slave owners.

On November 30, 1931, Coughlin attacked Hoover for his obstinate insistence that relief was a local matter, not the responsibility of the federal government. The radio priest pointed out that, in his own county, there had been a desperate need for milk for school children. His own Shrine of the Little Flower had donated $7,500 out of a needed $15,000, he said, but in an entire year the rest of the county had raised only $3,500. That was what was happening in a nation in which the government ladled out money to help stricken banks and railroads at the same time it was arguing that the starvation of the poor was a local matter!

There was much to be said for Father Coughlin's fiery attacks on the old order; but, like all demagogues, he did not know the meaning of responsibility and restraint. He flailed out in all directions, screaming as loudly for wrong causes as for good. Typical of his wildness was the manner in which he took up the cudgels for New York City's Mayor James J. Walker. Walker, a fellow Catholic, was under investigation by the Seabury Committee and Father Coughlin decided he was being crucified for his Catholicism, ignoring the abundant evidence that Walker had presided over one of the most corrupt regimes the great city had ever known. Father Coughlin's loud and irresponsible defense of Walker was coupled with an even more indefensible action. He lashed out at the upright former judge, Samuel Seabury, who was conducting the Walker investigation, as a bigot and a member of the Ku Klux Klan.

The Walker affair was a significant incident in the career of the radio priest who now spoke each Sunday to an estimated thirty million listeners. His hold on his followers was demonstrated each week by the number of bulging mail sacks that were delivered to his Royal Oak parish. The volume of mail was so overwhelming that he had to hire 106 clerks and four secretaries just to keep abreast of it. No doubt about it, he was a force.

His power to sway his vast radio audience made him an important figure in the Presidential campaign of 1932. Early in the campaign, Father Coughlin championed Governor Franklin D. Roosevelt, of New York, for the Democratic Presidential nomination; and, time and again, he coupled his attacks on President Hoover with the declaration that the only choice was "Roosevelt or Ruin." Roosevelt recognized his value, but handled him gingerly.

He exchanged polite letters with the radio priest. He greeted Father Coughlin cordially when they met. But he tried always to put a certain discreet distance between himself and his loudly vocal supporter. He commented to one aide, speaking of Father Coughlin: "We must tame these fellows and make them useful to us." And, according to Mrs. Roosevelt, he always "disliked and distrusted" the radio priest.

Roosevelt's caution was justified. It did not take Father Coughlin long to turn on the man he had supported. There seems to be little question that he had expected, just as Huey Long had expected, to have an important voice in the counsels of the new administration, but he gradually realized that he had no voice at all.

Father Coughlin continued to repeat his favorite phrase that it was "Roosevelt or Ruin," but he also began to snipe at Roosevelt's New Deal reforms. They did not begin to go far enough fast enough, he felt, to solve the problems of the depression. And so he began to develop his own cure-all for the nation's ills.

To the radio priest, the bankers represented the power of evil. He lashed out at the banking fraternity of Detroit, on the basis of no solid evidence whatsoever, as being composed essentially of a bunch of crooks. He was shocked that the Roosevelt Administration, in its first strenuous effort, concentrated on saving the privately owned banking system. The government, he felt, should take over the banks. Increasingly, he clamored for a program of inflation. The government should coin silver and issue more paper money, he declared; these steps would put more money into circulation and, at one stroke, solve the worst problems of the depression. He did not explain how this miracle would come about; he seemed to ignore the obvious—that inflation would drive up prices and do the poor more harm than good. More responsible men regarded such inflationary proposals with horror.

As the breach with the Roosevelt Administration widened, the President asked the post office to make a mail check to determine whether Father Coughlin really had the enormous following he claimed. The result must have been a shocker. The checkup showed that between July, 1933, and February, 1935, the Royal Oak Post Office had cashed 65,397 money orders worth $404,145 to the radio priest. And no one knew how many dollar bills came in that daily flood of mail or how many contributions had been made by check.

No one could doubt, however, that Father Coughlin was benefiting from a radio gold mine. Anyone who could see was convinced. The radio priest, who had started out with a flock of only twenty-five families in his parish, now was so wealthy he had erected a seven-story tower, with an immense crucified Christ across one side. In the tower were the offices of the Radio League of the Little Flower, Father Coughlin's personal headquarters, and offices for his large staff of helpers. And still there was enough money left over to pay, not only for the costs of his weekly radio broadcasts, but for the construction of a new Church of the Little Flower.

Such was the wealth and power of this unique radio demagogue as he neared his fateful break with Roosevelt. By the time he ended his radio season in April, 1934, Father Coughlin was close to taking this final step. In a letter to the members of his radio league, he referred to Roosevelt's celebrated Brain Trust as the "Drain Trust."

In the fall, he began his new radio series by saying he still supported the New Deal; but, just one week later, he denounced both political parties, declaring that their "putrefying carcasses" should be given "to the halls of a historical museum." He was still calling for a program to drive "the money changers from the temple." He was at war now with the whole capitalist system. "Capitalism is doomed and is not worth trying to save," he thundered. Finally, on November 11, 1934, he announced the formation of his own political organization—the National Union for Social Justice.

This was to be a "lobby for the people." But the people were not to have much to say about it. Members of the National Union were to be followers only. Father Coughlin, in what many saw as a fascist technique, would draw up "suitable" bills which would be presented to Congress and which all good members of the National Union would be pledged to support without question or dispute.

In his original announcement, Father Coughlin outlined a general, sixteen-point program. Many of his aims seemed moderate enough; others, more radical. But, whether moderate or radical, his program had a vagueness about it; he gave no hint, then or later, about the specific steps he proposed to make it work. He called for a guarantee of a "just, living, annual wage" for everyone wanting a job. He demanded the abolition of the privately owned banking system. He called for the nationalization of "public resources which by their very nature are too important to be held in the control of private individuals." He favored "private ownership of all other property," but there seemed to be a catch to this since he also made it clear he believed in "controlling" property "for the public good."

Human rights should be placed above property rights, and the government's chief concern should be with the poor since "the rich have ample means of their own to care for themselves." In the event of war, he called for "a conscription of wealth as well as a conscription of men."

Much of this program sounded good to Father Coughlin's enormous listening audience. Here, it seemed, was a priest who was really doing battle for the little man, who was fighting the all-powerful "interests"; and the vagueness about the means to be taken to reach the ends, the one-man dictation of the program so comparable to fascism, did not register at once with the public. Father Coughlin seemed to be riding a great wave of popular approval; and, whether this went to his head or not, there was now no holding him.

He swung wildly, taking on foes in bunches. In his December 9, 1934, broadcast, he managed in just one half-hour to do all this: he attacked the ultraconservative, big-business dominated American Liberty League; he raked bankers over the coals once more; he delivered a blistering attack on William Cardinal O'Connell, of Boston, who had presumed to reprimand him—and he unveiled his own program for spending $10 billion on public works to bring back prosperity. His attack on Cardinal O'Connell was so bold it made Catholics gasp. The Cardinal, said Father Coughlin, had been for forty years "more notorious for his silence on social justice than for any contribution" he had made toward correcting injustices and helping the poor.

The spectacle of a humble priest in a tiny Michigan parish defying such a high prelate of the church astounded many. Father Coughlin could get away with it for only

two reasons: he contended that, in pleading for social justice, he was carrying out church policy as laid down by
two Popes; and he had the full support of his own immediate superior, Bishop William J. Gallagher, of Detroit.
Since he was in Bishop Gallagher's diocese, he was safe as
long as the bishop backed him. Safe and free to go charging off in all directions.

It would be impossible to list all his targets, but here are
some of the things he did and said in the next few years:

* He attacked the great DuPont munitions and manu-
facturing family as "Merchandisers of Death."

* He proclaimed that capitalism and democracy were
both doomed. They would have to be replaced by "social
justice," but this was an ideal, not a political system, and
he never did explain how it would work.

* When President Roosevelt urged that the United
States join the World Court, hoping to make this nation's
influence felt in international affairs before the world was
dragged into another war, Father Coughlin attacked the
plan as "a stupid betrayal." His followers deluged the Senate with some 40,000 telegrams, and the World Court
proposal was defeated.

* He became ever more of an isolationist, opposing
every step taken by the Roosevelt Administration to pre-
pare the nation for World War II.

* He accused President Roosevelt of having communis-
tic leanings—and then, in the same program, almost in the
next breath, he belabored the President as the tool of capitalism.

* He denounced all labor unions, a most peculiar stand
for the champion of the working man; he employed non-
union labor on his construction projects in Royal Oak;

and, for years, his printed literature came from a non-union shop.

* When President Roosevelt urged Congress to pass a reorganization bill, much needed to streamline executive departments and bring about greater efficiency, Father Coughlin shouted that FDR wanted to become a dictator, and he made the extreme and silly charge that the President intended to seize all Catholic schools if the bill passed. Thousands of telegrams (ten thousand were sent from Detroit alone) swamped Congress, and the reorganization measure was defeated.

* He became increasingly a hate-monger. Though he always denied he was a man of racial hate, his actions belied his words. Jews were barred from membership in Social Justice Councils; Father Coughlin set up an organization known as the Christian Front, which had definite anti-Semitic overtones; and in July, 1938, his news sheet, *Social Justice*, published *The Protocols of Zion*. This tract purported to reveal a Jewish plot to take over the world; it had long been exposed as a fraud. But it was a favorite of hate-mongers, having been widely used by the Ku Klux Klan in the 1920s.

* And, finally, tied in with all of these revealing attitudes, was Father Coughlin's fondness for fascist dictators. He supported Italian dictator Benito Mussolini's seizure of Ethiopia; on occasion, he glorified Adolf Hitler; he enthusiastically endorsed Hitler and Mussolini when they established Francisco Franco as the dictator of Spain during the Spanish Civil War.

The demagoguery, the half-baked solutions to crucial problems and the appeals to passion all came to a head in the political campaign of 1936. On June 19, in a radio broadcast to his thirty million listeners, Father Coughlin put his movement into national politics. It was significant, as always, that this was a one-man deed; that he alone decided, announced, took action. His followers were *told;* they were not consulted.

In savage terms, Father Coughlin attacked Roosevelt and the New Deal. His motto, "Roosevelt or Ruin," now became "Roosevelt *and* Ruin." Therefore, he said, he was announcing the formation of a new party—the Union Party. It would have a candidate for President—Representative William Lemke, a North Dakota Republican with a personal following in the farm states. It would have the support of two other fanatic groups: the remnants of Huey Long's Share Our Wealth movement, now under the leadership of Gerald L. K. Smith, one of the most violent anti-Semites in the nation; and the followers of Dr. Francis Townsend, who advocated pensions for the elderly.

Father Coughlin had at last abandoned sideline sniping and entered the big leagues, inviting a showdown with the powerful Republican and Democratic parties. He evidently thought that all he had to do was to announce his purpose, to make a few spellbinding speeches—and those millions of radio listeners would automatically flock into the polling booths and vote for Lemke. He did not expect actually to elect Lemke, but he apparently expected to get Lemke so many votes Roosevelt could not win a majority. In that event, the Presidential choice would be thrown into the House of Representatives, where almost anything could happen. Father Coughlin was so carried away with this vision of his personal power that he pledged to leave the air if Lemke did not receive at least nine million votes.

The campaign for Lemke was marked by excess piled

upon excess. On July 16, Father Coughlin spoke to 10,000 Townsend Plan delegates at their convention in Cleveland. He whipped them into a frenzy. He called Roosevelt that "great betrayer and liar." He became so carried away that he ripped off his coat and clerical collar as he poured it on. The 10,000 Townsendites roared and applauded, then paraded for an hour in his honor.

This show was an example of the kind of passions a skilled demagogue can arouse, but it was a pale performance beside what happened in Cleveland a month later. The occasion was the convention of the National Union for Social Justice, and the issue was simple: the convention was assembled to ratify Father Coughlin in his deeds and confirm him in his leadership. In a column in *Social Justice* prior to the convention, Father Coughlin put the choice squarely to his disciples. They could make him just "a Victrola disk" if they wished, they could "relegate me to the graveyard of 'has-beens' "—or they could approve of him and all his works.

When he spoke to a massive crowd of 42,000 of the faithful, he quickly demonstrated, as author Wallace Stegner later wrote, "that he was one of the most effective speakers alive." Stegner added: "When he called for clapping as a sign of approval, the sound was deafening; when he called on those who agreed to stand up, the audience rose in one surging wave. And most effective of all devices: seven minutes before the scheduled end of his address, he wavered, staggered, collapsed, and was helped off by a group of grim-faced guards. Whether this collapse came from heat, indigestion, or histrionics, it couldn't have been better timed. The lady who had the honor of proposing Father Coughlin's name for the presidency of

the National Union almost swooned herself at the enor-
mity of her mission. Her nomination was unanimously
approved—or almost unanimously. At the crucial moment a malcontent delegate named O'Donnell rose and
bawled, 'No!' and was escorted out by police in imminent
danger of his life."

The campaign went on and on, with Father Coughlin
arousing passions wherever he went. He called the Republican Presidential candidate, Governor Alfred M. Landon,
of Kansas, "a menace" and predicted revolution if Landon
were elected. He called Roosevelt a Communist. In Boston, he got into an unpriestly brawl with a reporter, John
Barry, and the New York *Daily News* published a picture
showing him in the act of punching Barry in the nose. All
this fury, all these wild-swinging appeals came to nothing.

The colorless William Lemke got, not nine million
votes, but a mere 892,000, less than 2 per cent of the
national total. He did not carry a single state. Roosevelt,
in a fantastic landslide, swept every state in the union
except Maine and Vermont.

What had happened is what has so often happened in
America. When Americans went to the polling booths,
they obviously decided not to waste their votes for a third-
party candidate who had no chance; they decided to vote
on a practical level for the one of the two leading candidates who, they thought, would be better for them. By so
deciding, they also repudiated Father Coughlin's passion-
peddling. As so often happens in America, an extremist
orator may arouse his audiences to fever pitch, but out
across the nation, among the great mass of the people, he
alarms and turns off many thousands more than he per-
suades.

And so Father Coughlin's political adventure was dead. Faithful to his promise to retire from radio in such an event, he bid a sad farewell to his listening audience.

But he could not stay silent for long. He continued to lash out at the Roosevelt Administration in the pages of *Social Justice*. And after his great supporter, Bishop Gallagher, died suddenly in January, 1937, he went back on the air—his excuse and justification the contention that one of the dying bishop's last requests was that he resume his broadcasts.

The Catholic Church now belatedly tried to restrain him, and there was a succession of on-again, off-again radio performances. Now, you heard Father Coughlin; now, you didn't. But whenever he was heard, the voice was the same, warm and persuasive; the appeal was the same—to emotion, to prejudice, to hate.

No major radio network, no leading station in the largest cities would now carry his diatribes. In 1938 he put together a string of forty-six smaller, independent stations, but he had none west of Kansas or south of Maryland. He implied that the reason he had such trouble getting on the air was that the Jews controlled CBS, NBC, Mutual, and WOR. He announced that he agreed with the Nazi theory that the Jews had brought about the Russian Revolution in 1917 and had held twenty-four of the top twenty-five posts in the Bolshevik regime of Lenin.

This broadcast touched off another wave of sound and fury. Radio Station WMCA in New York, which had aired the speech, was horrified at its historical inaccuracies. The station said it had pointed these out to Father Coughlin before the broadcast, but he had refused to correct his script. The station asked that his future utterances be submitted to it forty-eight hours before air time for clearance; he refused. He said his speeches were being cleared by Catholic censors—a contention, never denied, that implicated the high command of the church in his hate-mongering. WMCA then refused to carry the broadcasts. When it did, violence erupted. Legions of street hoodlums now belonged to Father Coughlin's Christian Front, and these young thugs picketed the station, brawled with and beat up their critics, many of them Jews. Violence became almost commonplace on the streets of New York, and there were numerous complaints that the city's largely Irish-Catholic police force was dragging its feet in restraining Christian Front strong-arms.

The evil of it all is perhaps best capsuled in the story of what happened to one man. Wallace Stegner later described how a Russian-Jewish picture framer whom he called Ben Levin made the journey from dedicated follower to victim. Levin lived in Mattapan, Massachusetts, a suburb of Boston. When he first heard Father Coughlin lashing out at the "money changers," it seemed to him that the radio priest made sense. Father Coughlin seemed to him the only man "with the guts to speak out," and he put a dollar in an envelope, mailed it to Royal Oak, and became a member of the Radio League of the Little Flower.

But when Father Coughlin attacked President Roosevelt as a "betrayer and liar," Ben Levin began to worry. He wrote the priest, asking him to explain why he had made such a remark. Coughlin half-apologized in *Social Justice*, saying he had been carried away when he used the word "liar," but then he in effect repeated the offense by saying Roosevelt hadn't always told the truth. Ben Levin was troubled, but he continued to work for Coughlin's Union Party almost up to election day. The longer the campaign went on, however, the more disturbed Ben Levin had become. He did not like it when Father Coughlin in Cincinnati referred to Roosevelt as "anti-God." He did not like the way Father Coughlin, just like the Nazis, labeled every liberal a Communist or the way he talked as if the great labor union, the Congress of Industrial Organizations, was run directly from Moscow. And it really all became too much when Father Coughlin advocated the use of bullets "when any upstart dictator in the United States succeeds in making a one-party government and when the ballot becomes useless." In the end, Ben Levin, like millions of others, voted for Roosevelt.

In 1938, when Father Coughlin went all-out in his Jew-baiting, Ben Levin quickly felt the effects. Followers of the radio priest would come into his shop, stick a Jew-baiting issue of *Social Justice* under his nose, and say: "Here, you're a Jew, Levin. You ought to read what your pals have been doing lately. Take a look how your investments in Russia are coming."

After the outbreak of World War II in Europe, the ugly situation became uglier still. Father Coughlin's pro-Nazi youth gangs roamed the streets of a dozen cities. They terrorized Jewish sections. Mothers became afraid to send their children to school because young hoodlums, encouraged by their Christian Front elders, made a practice of beating up any Jewish boy they could catch alone. In Mattapan, the Coughlinites didn't kid Ben Levin any more; they didn't stick issues of *Social Justice* under his nose. They simply wrecked his shop. Finally, in the fall of 1941, after his shop had been demolished for the third time, Ben

Levin was put out of business; he simply had to give up, and he took a job in downtown Boston.

With the United States itself at war after the Japanese attack on Pearl Harbor, support of the Axis powers came close to treason. In April, 1942, Attorney General Francis Biddle charged *Social Justice* with violations of the Espionage Act, and the Postmaster General banned it from the mails. Father Coughlin's followers erupted in flurries of violence, but the priest himself decided not to fight the case in the courts and *Social Justice* folded.

That marked the final eclipse of Father Coughlin. He remained for years the priest of tiny Royal Oak parish; but his National Union for Social Justice was dissolved, he vanished from the radio, his name was rarely mentioned— almost, indeed, forgotten. But the evil he had done lived on. He had fed the grass roots of hate in America, and the hate survived even in wartime, even when Jews like other Americans were fighting and dying for their country. As Wallace Stegner wrote:

". . . The beatings of Jewish children in Dorchester and Mattapan and the Bronx and Brooklyn and Philadelphia went on. Ben Levin's oldest son raised up on a patrol on Guadalcanal and took a Japanese rifle bullet between the eyes; a few months later his youngest brother was run off a South Boston beach by a gang of Irish kids who taunted him with what would happen to the cowardly Jews as soon as the war was over. And this was not a propaganda story devised by a do-good organization to show the evils of race feeling. This was sober truth. This happened to real people. I have talked a good deal with Ben Levin and Ben Levin's youngest son, and I have inspected the official announcement of the oldest son's death and fingered his Purple Heart."

Such are the wages of racial hate. Such were the seeds Father Coughlin had sowed. The radio priest himself had been silenced; he had faded into the shadows of that obscurity from which he had sprung. But he had injected millions with the virus of suspicion and hate—and that is a long-lasting virus. It may lie quietly in the blood stream of a nation for years, but it does not go completely away. It is still there, and it can still be tapped, as it was soon to be in this case, by a demagogue more menacing and more powerful than Father Coughlin had ever been.

7

SENATOR JOE McCARTHY

The decade of the 1950s was made to order for a demagogue. It was a time when all America ran scared.

Physically, there was no reason that this should have been so. The sickness was all in the mind—in the minds of the leaders and the minds of the people.

Compared to the depression-wracked 1930s, the decade of the 1950s seemed almost like utopia achieved. The United States had emerged from World War II as the strongest nation on earth. It was a nation that had done what no nation had ever done before; it had fought powerful enemies on both sides of the globe, in Europe and in Asia, and it had crushed both. Enormous wartime production had brought with it an unrivaled prosperity. The average working man had an income and comforts and possessions, which he had not even dreamed of in the 1930s. Yet the nation was sick with suspicion and fear.

The mood resulted in part from the violent overthrow of certain very important expectations. Almost everyone had supposed that victory in World War II would bring peace—a peace that might last for generations. But the war had hardly ended when it was succeeded by a time of near-war tension that became known as the Cold War.

Russia, our wartime ally, became suddenly Russia, our peacetime enemy. Tensions had begun to develop even before the war in Europe had ended. The Russian armies swept over Poland and the Balkan states, gobbling up huge sections of Eastern Europe, threatening the rest. Less than two weeks after President Franklin D. Roosevelt's death in April, 1945, President Harry S. Truman defied and upbraided the Russians—and the Cold War, in effect, was on. It grew in intensity with each passing year.

The year 1949 has been labeled by Professor Eric F. Goldman, of Princeton University, a historical expert, "the year of shocks." China fell to the Communists, and Chiang Kai-shek, the wartime ruler of China whom we had supported, fled to the off-coast island of Formosa. Hardly had this happened when Russia exploded an atomic bomb. We had thought that, in the atomic bomb, we had had a scientific secret that we could keep for fifteen to twenty years; but now, in just four, Russia had caught up to us. Russia, too, now had the dread weapon that could wipe out whole cities and hundreds of thousands of people in one blinding flash.

How had this all happened? How could so much have gone so wrong so rapidly? There was, it seemed, just one simple explanation: we had been betrayed. Spies and subversives—Communist fellow travelers in the highest positions in our government—had done us in. This appeared to many to be what *must* have happened.

The stage was perfectly set for the most powerful demagogue in American history—Senator Joseph R. McCarthy, a little-known Republican from Wisconsin.

Joe McCarthy, as he became known to millions of Americans, was a contradictory figure, two men in one. The first was a likable, back-slapping boon companion who wanted to be loved by everyone. The second—the man who emerged under opposition or threat—was a savage, scowling battler who stopped at nothing.

McCarthy was born November 14, 1908, on a worn-out farm in upper Wisconsin about a hundred miles north of Milwaukee. He worked his way through college and law school. In college, he was an amateur boxer, a crude and unskilled one who threw all science to the winds and charged headlong, with swinging, wild, windmill blows. As a young lawyer, his earnings were small, and he played poker more than he worked at the law. He became known as a poker player who would bluff outrageously on every hand. Opponents never knew quite how to figure him. Just when they thought he must be bluffing again, he would come up with a pat hand and rake in a huge pot. These traits told much about Joe McCarthy; he was to remain all his life the reckless headlong battler—and master of the art of the colossal bluff.

In 1939 when he was thirty-one McCarthy joined the Republican Party in Wisconsin, and got himself elected as a circuit court judge. Just two years later the United States became involved in World War II, and he enlisted in the Marines, was commissioned a lieutenant, and went off to the South Pacific. He was an intelligence officer, assigned to secure rear bases, but sometimes, just for the fun of it, he rode in the tail-gunner's seat of a bomber on routine missions and blasted away at coconut trees. Ever a master at publicizing himself, he had his picture taken in combat uniform; copies flooded the Wisconsin newspapers; and, almost overnight, he became "Tail Gunner Joe"—a war hero.

The legend helped in 1946 when he ran for the U.S. Senate seat long held by Robert M. La Follette, Jr. La

Follette was the son of Wisconsin's most famous politician, "Fighting Bob" La Follette. The La Follette name was a household word in the state, and few gave upstart young Joe McCarthy a fighting chance.

But times were changing. Even so soon after the war, the jitters were setting in. Russia had become a menace. Things had obviously gone wrong. Republicans throughout the 1946 campaign raised a great hue and cry against Communists and fellow travelers in the Democratic Administration in Washington. La Follette, though running in the Republican primary in Wisconsin, had a liberal voting record, having sided on critical issues with the Democratic Administration. The result was that La Follette found he had enemies on all sides. Conservative Republicans detested him for his liberalism. And Communists, then strong in some of Wisconsin's labor unions, hated him even more viciously because he had delivered one of the first Cold War speeches in the Senate, denouncing Russia as a menace to world peace. The situation was tailor-made for Joe McCarthy. He attacked La Follette sometimes as a pro-Fascist type; at other times, in utter contradiction, as a Communist fellow traveler. Enough of the wild charges stuck so that La Follette lost his usual strong backing in the big-city labor wards; and brash Joe McCarthy, scoring an upset of upsets, went to Washington as the new U.S. senator from Wisconsin.

As a freshman senator, McCarthy built a record of dubious value. He became known as the lobbyists' best friend. He accepted a $10,000 check from a manufacturer of prefabricated homes for trumpeting the virtues of such housing at the same time he was supposed, in his official capacity, to be investigating housing. He developed a close relationship with a Pepsi-Cola lobbyist who signed a $20,000 note for him—and he battled in the Senate to get postwar sugar rationing relaxed so that Pepsi-Cola could get more sugar. Even worse, he injected himself into a Senate investigation of the World War II Malmedy massacre. It was at Christmastime, 1944, that Nazi storm troopers machine-gunned one hundred helpless Belgian civilians and one hundred fifty captured American soldiers in the little crossroads Belgian town of Malmedy. After the war, several of the Nazi murderers were arrested, tried, and convicted. Then a publicity campaign began in Germany in an effort to save their lives. Back home in Wisconsin, McCarthy had had heavy backing among neo-Nazi elements; and so, though he was not a member of the Senate committee investigating the Malmedy atrocity, he took an active hand in the probe. And he wound up attacking American Army officers, contending they had tortured the Nazis to obtain forced confessions. His tactics disrupted the hearings; and, in Germany, the Communist press had a field day slandering America and Americans. The death sentences of the condemned Nazis were finally commuted.

Up to 1950, then, the McCarthy record was hardly admirable. He had become the bosom pal of lobbyists. He had defended the Nazi murderers of Malmedy—and played into the hands of German Communists in doing so. It was not a record with which a politician could go back before his constituents, seeking re-election in 1952. McCarthy needed an issue.

He was hunting for one that would put his name in headlines. And in January, 1950, at dinner with some friends in Washington's swank Colony Restaurant, several ideas were batted around unenthusiastically until finally someone suggested the Communist issue. McCarthy seized upon the idea at once and asked the Republican National Committee to arrange some speaking dates for him during the annual Lincoln Day party rallies taking place across the nation.

McCarthy was not well enough known at the time to rate major speaking engagements, and so the committee sent him off to Wheeling, West Virginia. It was there on February 9, 1950, at a Republican rally, that he delivered the speech that was to make him known in every household in America. One paragraph, one gesture stood out. McCarthy was quoted as saying:

"While I cannot take time to name all the men in the State Department who have been named as members of the Communist Party and members of a spy ring, *I have here in my hand* a list of 205 that were known to the secretary of state as being members of the Communist Party and who, nevertheless, are still working and shaping policy in the State Department."

It was a statement that touched off a frenzy. It was the charge that launched the worst witch hunt this nation has ever known.

Why should those few lines of type, why should that gesture of a paper waved aloft in clenched hand, have sent an entire nation down the road of a kind of mass insanity, hunting for Communists under every bed? The timing of the charge helps to explain the mass explosion.

Republicans had been trying for years to tar the liberal regimes of Presidents Franklin D. Roosevelt and Harry S. Truman with a Communist affiliation. They had struggled desperately to make the propaganda stick in the Presidential campaign of 1948—and had failed by an eyelash. They had concentrated most of their fire on Alger Hiss, a brilliant young aide in the State Department; Whittaker Chambers, a confessed former Communist, charged that Hiss had passed him official papers to send to Russia. It was an infinitely complicated, mysterious case; but, finally, after two trials, Alger Hiss had been convicted of perjury on January 25, 1950, just fifteen days before McCarthy spoke at Wheeling. And this was not all.

Even as McCarthy was speaking, the British press was announcing the arrest of Klaus Fuchs. Fuchs, a refugee scientist who had been cleared by British security, had been sent here during wartime to work on the development of the atom bomb. And now Fuchs confessed that he had been spying for Russia and had passed along information through a Communist spy ring operating in this country. Spies. Subversion. The "secret" of the atom bomb gone to Russia. Here was tinder waiting to set off a conflagration; and, at exactly the right minute, Joe McCarthy came along and applied the torch.

He did not realize at once what a good thing he had. There are even some indications he may have been a bit scared himself at first, for as he continued on West on his Lincoln Day tour, reporters began to ask him about that 205 figure he had used at Wheeling, and McCarthy at first tried to back off. He didn't think he had used such a figure, he said, but it didn't matter really, he was certain there were enough Communists in the State Department to betray the nation.

In Salt Lake City two days after Wheeling, the 205 Communists had shrunk to 57, a figure that was still startling enough. And McCarthy was positive—oh, so positive

—about those. He told a radio interviewer (his words were preserved on tape) that, if Secretary of State Dean Acheson "wants to call me tonight at the Utah Hotel, I will be glad to give him the names of those fifty-seven card-carrying Communists." He added: "I don't want to indicate there are only fifty-seven, I say I have the names of fifty-seven."

As it became more and more evident that he had touched a quaking nerve in the nation, he became incredibly brash. He fired off a telegram to President Truman, challenging him to a duel of truth about those fifty-seven Communists he said were making policy in the State Department. And, on his return to Washington, he took the Senate floor late in the afternoon of February 20, 1950, and in a long, rambling speech, he indicted the Truman Administration for having permitted wholesale penetration and subversion of executive departments by Communists. But the figures had changed again. The number of Communists boring from within was no longer 205 or 57; it was now 81.

Even this new and revised tally would not stand close examination. Although McCarthy claimed to be citing specific cases, an analysis of the speech shows that McCarthy couldn't add. He didn't have eighty-one cases. He skipped some case numbers completely. He dragged in others even though he admitted himself that they did *not* involve Communist activities. Sometimes he duplicated, and once he even caught himself in the act, confessing: "I believe I have covered this case before, and what I have just said seems to be a repetition. . . ."

When McCarthy had finished, even Senator Robert A. Taft, the conservative "Mr. Republican" of his party, admitted: "It was a perfectly reckless performance." But the Democrats, amazingly, had sat on their hands throughout those long hours while McCarthy ranted and raved and exposed himself as a perfect target for their fire. They badgered him about the 205 figure he had used at Wheeling, but they made no serious attack on his shot-full-of-holes recital. Why? Political observers speculated then and later that the Democrats' faith in themselves and their party had been destroyed by the Hiss case—a case which McCarthy and Republican orators repeatedly cited as the proof of everything—and so they hesitated to challenge McCarthy's thesis that there were any number of other Hisses running loose in the State Department.

McCarthy was certainly a vulnerable politician. His fellow senators knew full well his reputation as "the water boy of the real estate lobby," the bosom pal of Pepsi-Cola, the defender of the Nazi murderers of Malmedy. Yet they accorded him full respect as a statesman; they promised a full-fledged investigation of his charges before a subcommittee of the Senate Foreign Relations Committee—and so they collaborated in ratifying in the public mind the suspicion that Joe McCarthy must have something.

Senator Millard F. Tydings, an extremely conservative Maryland Democrat whom President Roosevelt had once tried to purge from the party, headed the investigation. He made the mistake of trying to hound McCarthy at the start, badgering him about the Wheeling figure of 205 Communists, and McCarthy turned the hearing into a shambles. Tydings' obvious hostility gave him an ace in the hole, and he played it like the cagey poker player he was. Tydings, he shouted, was not trying to find out about Communists in the State Department; he was trying to pillory Joe McCarthy. Donning martyr's robes, McCarthy proclaimed that the whole Tydings inquiry would be a partisan whitewash, and he shouted this "whitewash" charge so long and so loudly that a good portion of the nation came to believe him.

It simply did not register with the public that McCarthy offered no proof of any of his charges. He avoided proof by contending it was up to the committee to investigate and find the proof. He even denied he was making charges, though obviously he was; he was simply, he said, bringing "a situation" to the committee's attention. No sooner had one of his headline cases collapsed (and they did one after another) than he produced a new and more sensational one. And newspaper headlines concentrated on the new charges rather than the collapse of the old.

The Tydings committee eventually turned in a report, branding McCarthy's charges "a hoax and a fraud." But McCarthy, by this time, had so damaged the committee with his "whitewash" charges that its report had little effect, and it was adopted in the Senate on a strict party-line vote, Democrats aligned against Republicans, all of whom in the showdown ranged themselves behind the new demagogue from the Midwest.

The unceasing sound and fury in the headlines now was making McCarthy a national figure. Ultraconservative business interests for years had been trying to discredit the Roosevelt and Truman administrations by equating liberalism with communism, and here was the crier of alarm who was making their case stick with the public. Bulging wallets across the nation fell open, and money poured in to McCarthy to help him in his great "crusade."

The "crusade's" first target was Senator Tydings. Mc-

Carthy had been stung by the "hoax and fraud" pro-
nouncement. No one could do this to *him*. And so he went
into Maryland, hunting for Tydings' scalp.

He masterminded the Republican campaign against
Tydings, one of the dirtiest in American political history.
No blow was too low or too foul to be struck if it would
damage Tydings. A phony picture was distributed showing
Tydings and Communist leader Earl Browder smiling
fondly at one another. Subsequent investigation showed
that the picture was a composite that had been made by
taking two separate photographs—one of a smiling
Browder, another of a smiling Tydings—and rephoto-
graphing them together. The men had never met and
smiled at one another in such friendly fashion, but the
composite picture created the impression that they had.
Tydings was damaged and went down to defeat before his
little-known Republican opponent, and Joe McCarthy
rode higher than ever—a man who commanded such a
following he could defeat even Tydings, a senator who
had withstood the attack of Roosevelt and had been
elected again and again, almost without opposition.

Politicians got the message and quaked in their shoes.
Joe McCarthy was whipping the nation into a frenzy, con-
vincing millions that China had been "lost," that the secret
of the A-bomb had found its way into Russian hands because we had been betrayed. The Roosevelt and Truman
administrations, he thundered, represented "twenty years
of treason," and any politician who dared to oppose Joe
McCarthy automatically nominated himself for the designation of traitor.

This was a charge that appealed to emotions, that defied
reason and evidence. A man could deny he was a traitor;

he could protest his patriotism. But what good would that do? A traitor would naturally deny, protest; and in the atmosphere of the times, the louder one protested the more suspect one became.

The Presidential election of 1952 saw Joe McCarthy reaching a pinnacle of power. He had aroused such passions, he had gathered such a following that he became his party's ultimate weapon. General-hero Dwight D. Eisenhower was running for the Presidency on the high road, bathed in the sunshine of popular adoration—and there on the low road was Joe McCarthy, the unrivaled hatchetman, slashing away at the Democratic nominee, Governor Adlai Stevenson, of Illinois.

In speech after speech, McCarthy referred to Stevenson as "little Ad-lie." He suggested sometimes that he could "teach patriotism to little Ad-lie" if someone would only smuggle him aboard the Democratic campaign special with a baseball bat in his hands. Sometimes he would pretend to have made a slip, referring to Governor Stevenson as "Alger—I mean Ad-lie," his coy way of reminding his audiences of the Alger Hiss case.

In his attacks on various candidates that year he always flourished aloft his trademark—a sheaf of paper—and proclaimed that "I have here in my hand" proof of one kind or another. The "proof" might consist simply of the charge that the candidate he was attacking had belonged during the 1930s, in an entirely different era with entirely different problems, to some organization that had been adjudged some ten or fifteen years later to have been a "Communist front." Sometimes it wasn't even necessary for a man to have belonged himself; he might just have been a friend of someone who had belonged, or was said to have belonged—and so he was considered guilty by this association. However remote the tie might be, it was enough to give McCarthy the chance to flourish aloft his papers and rave about his "proof" that the candidate was a traitor or, at least, a tainted "fellow traveler."

When Eisenhower was elected in a landslide, Joe Mc-Carthy bestrode Capitol Hill, a figure of menace, the author of a nightmare. Before the election, many had reasoned that Eisenhower would be able to contain and restrain McCarthy as the Democrats could not. But it soon became obvious that the very opposite was true. McCarthy had been re-elected to the Senate in Wisconsin in the Eisenhower landslide; and when the Republicans took control of Congress, McCarthy was given power such as he had never had before. He was made chairman of the Senate Committee on Government Operations, with broad powers to investigate and with the command of an investigative staff.

Vice President Richard M. Nixon and others high in the Eisenhower Administration tried to persuade McCarthy to turn his energies to the probe of corruption in government, leaving the Communist issue to other Senate and House committees specifically set up for that purpose. But McCarthy was like a dog with his favorite bone. It was the Communist issue that had catapulted him from obscurity to national prominence, and he could not abandon the "crusade" that had made him famous. He had to get his name in ever bigger headlines. He had to keep on finding Communists—and more Communists. And so it was inevitable that the time would come, given this compulsion, when he would have to find Communists even in the Eisenhower Administration, when he would have to begin attacking his own Republican Administration even as he had attacked the Democrats.

Friends of America in Canada, England, France—in all the free nations of the world—were horrified at the spectacle. The most reliable estimates showed that fewer than 1 per cent of the American people were Communists. Yet here was the most powerful nation on earth, the nation that had been the birthplace of democracy, acting much as the Germans had acted when Hitler made the Jews the scapegoats for all his country's ills. McCarthy's roars terrified the entire Eisenhower Administration, and witch hunts spread as other unprincipled politicians tried to ape McCarthy's methods and capture for themselves some of his fame.

Writers who had joined left-wing causes in the 1930s to oppose Nazism and Fascism were hounded, their books banned. Painters and composers were tarred and discredited, as if their paintings and music had become somehow contaminated by their political beliefs. The State Department was completely demoralized. Secretary of State John Foster Dulles changed policies back and forth at the mere whisper of McCarthy's displeasure. The U.S. Information Agency, the propaganda arm of the department, was forbidden to quote Communist leaders like Stalin even when the purpose was to show that they had lied. Foreign Service officers, who had been investigated and cleared time and time again by the departmental security agency and the Federal Bureau of Investigation, were called on the carpet once more and dismissed despite the lack of any new or valid evidence, their careers ruined out of fear that, otherwise, McCarthy would blast the department as soft on Communism. Throughout the nation, the common

workingman—the butcher, plumber, electrician, factory
hand—had to be cleared of the faintest taint of suspicion
if he worked for the government or his firm held government contracts. So far did the madness go that even reading the *New York Times*, judged by practically all experts
to be the nation's leading newspaper, was enough to make
one suspect in some circles—especially since the *Times*
did not bow down to McCarthy.

Some of President Eisenhower's supporters advised him
repeatedly to confront McCarthy, to put an end to the
frenzy and the witch hunt. But the President refused, in-
sisting: "I just will not—*I refuse*—to get into the gutter
with that guy." It was clear that Eisenhower did not want
to fight, and it was just as clear that McCarthy was on a
collision course, that a battle to the political death would
be inevitable in the end.

The showdown came suddenly at a time when Mc-
Carthy seemed to be riding the crest of the wave of suspicion and frenzy he had created. It was largely the result of
the antics of two young assistants on McCarthy's staff—
Roy M. Cohn, whom McCarthy had named counsel of his
investigating committee, and G. David Schine, a staff investigator and close friend of Cohn. These two brought
McCarthy into direct conflict with one of the true power
complexes of the nation—the U.S. Army.

Cohn and Schine were both twenty-six. Cohn was so
brilliant he had whipped through college and Columbia
University Law School by the time he was nineteen, and
he had to wait two years to become of age before he could
take his bar examination. He was then appointed an Assistant U.S. Attorney in New York, and he began to investigate narcotics traffickers, counterfeiters, and, finally,
spies.

Schine was a tall, sleepily handsome young man, the heir to a great hotel fortune. He had written a sketchy treatise on Communism, which he had placed beside the Bibles in his family's hotels; and so he had come to the attention of Cohn and McCarthy and had been made a specialist in Communist investigations.

These two young men touched off the first wave of unfavorable publicity McCarthy had encountered. They toured Europe together at Easter time, 1953. Their purpose was to investigate the contents of U.S. overseas libraries, and they went to the kind of extremes that reminded many of the book purges in Germany during Hitler's time.

Cohn and Schine checked titles in U.S. libraries against those in Russian libraries. Obviously, if the Russians were displaying books we were also exhibiting, it might indicate that our book shelves were dangerously tainted. Applying this rule of thumb, they discovered that both U.S. and Russian libraries contained the works of Mark Twain. More sinister still was the case of Dashiell Hammett, the detective story writer. Hammett's political ideas were far to the left of what any good McCarthyite could consider acceptable—and yet there were his works, his Thin Man detective series, displayed on the shelves of U.S. libraries. Cohn and Schine were shocked not only at what they found, but at the absence of some far rightist literature on our library shelves. They upbraided one librarian because he had not stocked copies of two minor publications—*The Freeman*, an ultra-right propaganda sheet, and the *American Legion Magazine*.

This kind of intellectual witch-hunting was bad enough, but even more damage was done by the personal antics of Cohn and Schine. In one episode, Schine was reported to have chased Cohn around a hotel lobby, whacking at his rear with a rolled-up magazine. Though both denied the incident ever happened, it was widely reported in the world press as a fact, and it helped to make the United States the laughing stock of Europe.

The European tour of Cohn and Schine was followed by events that disgraced the United States as had nothing yet. Books that might offend the McCarthy witch hunters, including the detective stories of Dashiell Hammett, were removed from overseas library shelves. And in some cases books were actually burned. The number of volumes consigned to bonfires was minute, only a half-dozen or so, but it was the symbolism of the act that counted. Here were official agents of this supposedly great and free democracy doing just what the Nazis had done—destroying the works of authors they hated. Even President Eisenhower, who had gone to extremes to avoid a break with McCarthy, felt compelled to denounce book-burning as un-American, and Hammett's harmless detective stories and some other volumes that had been banned were brought out again into the light of day.

For the moment, it seemed, the showdown had been avoided; but all the time, behind the scenes, another drama was being enacted. In mid-July, 1953, the U.S. Army began threatening G. David Schine with induction into military service. Roy Cohn, according to the army, began a series of frantic maneuvers designed to get his friend favored treatment. Not only the army but every other branch of the armed services was badgered to obtain a commission for Schine, but none would give him officer status. Cohn, according to the army, was wildly furious, and on one occasion threatened to "get" the army.

Dovetailing with this secret struggle was a succession of public events. There would be much dispute later about whether the Cohn-Schine rumpus was to blame, but the fact remained that it was just at this time that McCarthy began a series of attacks on the army. His first target was the great Signal Corps laboratory complex at Fort Monmouth, New Jersey, where much of the advanced radar for World War II had been developed.

McCarthy bellowed his way into headlines day after day, charging that the Fort Monmouth installations were riddled with spies. He conducted a series of secret hearings in New York, beginning on October 3, 1953; and, after each hearing, he would come out and tell reporters what he had discovered. Since the press could not know what had actually taken place behind the closed doors of the hearing room, it had to take McCarthy's word for it—and McCarthy's words were always alarming and sometimes horrifying. Over and over again, he claimed that he had uncovered evidence of spy rings that were still active at Fort Monmouth.

None of it was true. It took months—in some cases, years—for his charges to be sifted, but in the end they collapsed utterly, every one of them. The commanding general of Fort Monmouth, looking back in 1969, reported that only seven employees had been suspended as "security risks," a designation that is much broader than a charge of espionage. A man may be a security risk if he is a drunk or a homosexual, or if he is chronically head-over-heels in debt. What was truly startling in the Fort Monmouth case, however, was that not even the security risk firings could be sustained. According to Maj. Gen. William B. Latta in 1969, all seven employees suspended as security risks "were reinstated eventually"—and this under a system in which the government needed only to establish that there was enough evidence against a man to create "a doubt" about the advisability of his continued employment. Even under these one-sided circumstances, with all the dice loaded against the accused employees, there had been absolutely nothing to support McCarthy's sensational charges.

This, of course, could not have been apparent at the time, and McCarthy, as was typical of him, went on to a new sensation before the public had a chance to catch its breath. He discovered finally, perhaps for the only time in his career, a man who apparently had been a Communist.

The suspect was Irving Peress, a New York City dentist who had been drafted on October 15, 1952, and had been stationed at Camp Kilmer, New Jersey, outside New Brunswick. In filling out his personnel forms, Peress had claimed the privilege of the Fifth Amendment against possible self-incrimination in answering questions about possible subversive activities and associations. This tell-tale stain went undetected for months in the flood of paper work that engulfed the Pentagon, and so on October 23, 1953, Peress was promoted to major. The promotion was not a personal reward; some 7,000 other doctors and dentists also received automatic promotions as provided by newly adopted regulations. But McCarthy, tipped to the possibilities of the Peress case, immediately summoned Peress to testify before him. Peress took the Fifth Amendment to thirty-two questions dealing with possible Communist affiliations, and McCarthy uttered a scream that made headlines across the nation: "Who promoted Peress?"

In an effort to answer the question, he summoned before him the commanding general of Camp Kilmer, Brig. Gen. Ralph W. Zwicker. Zwicker was a much-decorated hero of World War II. He had led a scouting force ashore in the early hours of the D-Day landing in Normandy. He had commanded a regiment of the Second Infantry Division in the Battle of the Bulge. There could be no question about his patriotism, but McCarthy treated him with contempt.

General Zwicker tried to explain that he had had nothing to say about the promotion of Peress. He had nothing to say about any case involving possible subversion. All such cases were referred to higher echelons in the Pentagon, where army intelligence specialists sifted the evidence and decisions were made as to what action should be taken. These decisions were relayed to General Zwicker through First Army Headquarters in New York. He was only the last man on the conveyor belt. None of this made any impression on McCarthy. He browbeat Zwicker unmercifully and finally denounced him as "unfit to wear that uniform."

This brazen slandering of a heroic general was too much. The Eisenhower Administration, which had sat still while the State Department was trampled underfoot, now was faced with an issue it could not dodge; if McCarthy was to be allowed to rage on unchecked in this fashion, the morale of the army also would be destroyed.

The first Republican to see and seize the issue was a much-respected senator from Vermont, Ralph W. Flanders. On March 9, Flanders took the floor of the Senate and flayed McCarthy unmercifully. He accused McCarthy of trying to set up "a one-man party, McCarthyism," and then he launched into this description of McCarthy in action:

"He dons his warpaint. He goes into his war dance. He emits his warwhoops. He goes forth to battle and proudly returns with the scalp of a pink army dentist. We may assume that this represents the depth and seriousness of the Communist penetration at this time."

Secretary of the Army Robert T. Stevens, a mild-mannered former textile manufacturer, had also become enraged. Stevens may have been no army expert, but he knew one thing: he could not permit his officers to be kicked around and insulted by McCarthy and still retain their respect or, more important, have any morale left in the army. And so he denounced McCarthy's methods and announced he would not permit army personnel to appear before McCarthy again and be subjected to such abuse.

The feud grew hotter with every uttered word. The army now leaked to the press the details of the way in which, it said, Cohn had badgered it to get a commission for Schine. It implied that McCarthy's investigations of the army were motivated by spite aroused by the Schine affair. McCarthy roared that Stevens was "a liar," and he accused the army of trying to "blackmail" him to call off his investigations. The conflict now was out in the open. It was so bitter there could be no compromise, and an investigation would have to be held to determine who was telling the truth.

A reluctant U.S. Senate ordered hearings, and these began in the full glare of television lights on April 22, 1954. It was a show that captured the attention of the entire nation. For the next several weeks, millions of Americans would eat their evening meals from television trays in their living rooms, their eyes glued to the evening newscasts, anxious not to miss a single act of the proceedings.

The setting, the personalities, the showdown nature of the issues—all were made to order for the kind of drama one usually sees only on the stage. The hearings were held in the plush Senate Caucus Room, its high ceiling supported by majestic columns, the scene of many stormy McCarthy hearings in the past. Senator Karl Mundt, a Republican from South Dakota, a long-time supporter of McCarthy, presided. The committee members sat in comfortable chairs on a raised dais behind a long, continuous judge's bench, the American flag draped in the background.

Before this row of judges, behind a long low counsel table, sat the contending parties. At one end was Joe McCarthy, dark-browed, sharp-nosed, a scowl on his swarthy features as he leaned his head sidewise to listen to the whispered words of Roy Cohn, who was serving as his personal counsel. Farther down the table was Ray H. Jenkins, fifty-seven, a rugged, square-jawed six-footer from Knoxville, Tennessee, the committee counsel.

Toward the other end of the table sat Secretary Stevens, stocky, solid-faced, unemotional; and beside him sat the man who was to become the star of the show—Joseph Nye Welch, a sixty-three-year old Boston lawyer who specialized in trial work. Welch was a chunky man with a deceptively pixie-like look about him. He had wide lips, a long face, a large broad nose, and high-arched quizzical eyebrows. He dressed like the proper Bostonian in conservative suits, little bow ties and vest. He seemed at times almost asleep, and he spoke in the softest tones. But his wit was rapier-sharp, and many a startled witness was to find that this mild-seeming man could skewer him with the harshest of harsh questions.

The hearing had hardly begun before Joe McCarthy propelled himself before the eyes of the watching television cameras.

"A point of order, Mr. Chairman, may I raise a point of order?" he cried in his shrill voice.

His objection was a highly technical one. Welch, he said, had represented himself as counsel for the army, and McCarthy contended Welch did not represent the army, but Stevens personally. The whole point seemed a bit silly, but McCarthy argued it as if the fate of the nation were at stake. Mundt finally cut him off and ordered Jenkins to call his first witness.

The brief flareup had served, however, to put Joe McCarthy immediately in the spotlight. It had given the public the first glimpse of McCarthy in action, and his cry—"Point of order, Mr. Chairman"—was one that was to be raised so incessantly in the coming days that it became in time a phrase of ridicule.

The hearings lasted for thirty-six days and amassed two million words of testimony. And, though many impressions were created, one came to dominate them all—the picture of Joe McCarthy snarling, ramping, raging, injecting himself into every scene, trying any dirty trick that he thought might work, and crying over and over again, "Point of order, Mr. Chairman."

Typical of his methods was his introduction of a picture doctored to create a false impression, just as the Tydings-Browder composite picture had been used in Maryland. Secretary Stevens was on the stand. He testified that "Senator McCarthy or members of his staff" made "more than sixty-five telephone calls" trying to get favored treatment for Private Schine. There was, he said, no other case "that matches this persistent, tireless effort to obtain special privileges and consideration for this man."

McCarthy hectored and hounded the secretary, trying to get him to admit that the army had held Schine as a kind of "hostage," its treatment of him depending on whether McCarthy would drop his investigations of the army. Secretary Stevens denied this. Schine had not been commissioned, he testified, because he did not qualify for a commission.

In the midst of this lengthy wrangle, Committee Counsel Ray Jenkins sprang a surprise. He asked Stevens whether he had ever asked to have his picture taken with Private Schine after Schine had been inducted into service at Fort Dix, New Jersey. The secretary seemed puzzled. He said army photographers were always snapping pictures when he visited various bases; his picture might have been taken with Schine; he couldn't recall.

Jenkins bored in. Had the secretary ever said, "I want my picture taken with David" and had it done?

"I am sure I never made a statement just like you made there," Stevens told him.

Jenkins whipped out a picture and shoved it under Stevens' nose. It showed the secretary and Private Schine posing happily together, just the two of them, smiling at each other. Jenkins stressed they were "alone." Wasn't this buddy-buddy picture evidence that Secretary Stevens had been "especially nice and considerate of this boy Schine?"

"Positively and completely not," Stevens declared.

This scene took place on the late afternoon of April 26,

1954; and when the hearing closed at this point, it seemed that the McCarthy forces had scored. The next morning, the whole complexion of the issue suddenly changed.

Joseph Welch strode before the eyes of the TV cameras and made his first impact on the watching millions. He charged that Jenkins "yesterday was imposed upon, and so was the Secretary of the Army, by having a doctored and altered photograph produced in this courtroom as if it were honest."

Welch now produced the original picture. It did not show Secretary Stevens and Schine "alone." It showed them standing with a third man, Air Force Colonel Jack T. Bradley, and the sleeve of a fourth appeared at the outer edge of the picture. This was obviously a group photograph that had been cropped deliberately to create a false impression.

"Mr. Chairman, a point of order," McCarthy cried.

He raged that Welch "makes a completely false statement that this [the original picture] is a group picture." Welch, he said, was "lying." On and on he raged, trying to turn the clear facts of the case upside down.

The committee devoted hours to tracing the spoor of the spurious picture. The original photograph had hung on Schine's office wall in New York. Cohn had told Jenkins about it. Private Schine had been dispatched to get the picture and bring it to Washington. "He procured the picture," Cohn testified. "He brought it down. I did not see it."

The picture had passed through several hands. Everyone concerned declared they had never even glanced at it. But the committee finally tracked the mystery down to the one man who had to know. He was James Juliana, a former FBI agent who had been employed as an investigator by the McCarthy committee. Juliana admitted he had taken the original picture and had given orders to have two sets of blowups made—one of the "group" picture and one cropped to show just Stevens and Schine "alone." He had put the group picture in the files and had given the "alone" shot to Cohn. Why had he done this? He had been under the impression that "Jenkins and/or Cohn" wanted "just a picture of Secretary Stevens and Private Schine."

Joseph Welch affected a gentle bewilderment as he took Juliana over the high hurdles. Was it Roy Cohn who had wanted the "alone" picture? Juliana protested that he did not "know," that this was an "unfair" question. But certainly, said kindly Joseph Welch, Juliana could testify about his "understanding" of the matter.

WELCH: When you leaned over to tell this glad, good news to Mr. Cohn, were you under the impression that he was hoping to hear you had a picture of the Secretary and Private Schine alone?

JULIANA: I was under the impression that this was glad news to Mr. Cohn . . .

The damage that this was doing was obvious to all, and McCarthy could restrain himself no longer. He made the fatal mistake of trying to match wits with Joseph Welch and touched off an exchange that sent a shock wave of mocking laughter across the land. Welch, in pursuit of Juliana, had finally gotten the badgered and hapless witness to say in confusion that he didn't know what the original picture from Schine's office wall had shown. In mock amazement, Welch flourished the original picture and asked:

"Did you think this came from a pixie? Where did you think this picture that I hold in my hand came from?"

"I had no idea," Juliana murmured.

Here McCarthy charged to the rescue.

"Will counsel for my benefit define—I think he might be an expert on that—what a pixie is?"

Lightning fast came Welch's rejoinder:

"Yes, I should say, Mr. Senator, that a pixie is a close relative of a fairy.

"Shall I proceed, sir? Have I enlightened you?"

As a gale of laughter swept the hearing room, Roy Cohn sat white-lipped and angry; McCarthy glowered— and a nation that had been terrorized by the grand inquisitor now began to find him ridiculous and to laugh.

The hearings went on and on, it seemed almost endlessly. McCarthy hounded Secretary Stevens for fourteen days. Though every question that could possibly be asked had been asked and answered, McCarthy insisted, when his turn for questioning came, on going over the same old ground again and again. The strain upon the secretary was evident. He became gray-faced under the glaring television lights; his right eye sometimes blinked uncontrollably; and his right cheek twitched.

Through it all, there was another major furor when McCarthy, in cross-examining Stevens, flashed what purported to be an FBI report, dated October 26, 1951, warning of possible espionage dangers at Fort Monmouth. How had McCarthy obtained an FBI "top secret" report? Was it genuine?

These questions occupied the committee for days. It

finally developed that the McCarthy report was not a copy
of the FBI original. It was a digest of a longer FBI document. And there was one striking difference between the
two. The FBI report had not attempted to judge; it had
merely recited what information had been obtained about
various employees. McCarthy's version, however, had the
word "derogatory" printed after some of the names.

In the uproar over this report, McCarthy brashly and
arrogantly announced that he would get and use "top
secret" government documents as he saw fit. He even appealed to "loyal" government employees to rifle the files
and send him any information they thought he should
have. This was anarchy. This was the supreme demagogue
setting himself above all rules and regulations, making all
government subject to his whim.

The dispute over the purloined and abbreviated FBI
report led to the final, climactic scene. The hearings would
drag on after it, twitching in a kind of final dying agony,
but after this one unforgettable moment, nothing else
really mattered.

This highlight came on June 9, 1954, while Welch was
cross-examining Roy Cohn. Welch established that Cohn
and McCarthy had had their version of the FBI report in
their possession for months, yet they hadn't informed Secretary Stevens in their own Republican Administration
about it. Welch asked Cohn why.

WELCH: And on September 7 when you met him [Sec-
retary Stevens] you had in your bosom this alarming situation about Monmouth, is that right?

COHN: Yes, I knew about Monmouth then, yes, sir.

WELCH: And you didn't tug his lapel and say, "Mr.

Secretary, I know something about Monmouth that won't let me sleep nights?"

COHN: I don't know.

WELCH: You didn't do it, did you?

COHN: I don't, as I have testified, Mr. Welch, I don't know whether I talked to Mr. Stevens about it then or not. . . .

Welch wanted to know if Cohn had any doubts about Stevens' fidelity. "No, sir." Or his honor? "No, sir." Or his patriotism? "No, sir." Welch drove home his point. "And yet, Mr. Cohn, you didn't tell him what you knew?" Cohn could only repeat helplessly that he did not know.

Then Welch, in his most puckish manner, suggested that when one had such information one should move "before sundown" to do something about it. "May I add my small voice, sir," he said in his gently sarcastic way, "and say whenever you know about a subversive or a Communist or a spy, please hurry. Will you remember those words?"

Ridicule is the deadliest weapon, and Joe McCarthy could no longer restrain himself.

"Point of order," he cried, and he charged one last fatal time before the television cameras.

"In view of Mr. Welch's request that information be given," he began, "I think we should tell him that he has in his law firm a young man named [Frederick H.] Fisher whom he recommended, incidentally, to do the work on this committee, who has been for a number of years a member of an organization which was named . . . as the legal bulwark of the Communist Party. . . ."

Roy Cohn sat slumped in the witness chair, shaking his

head in silent protest, but McCarthy charged recklessly on. He explained that Fisher had belonged to the National Lawyers Guild, an organization that had been labeled subversive by the House Un-American Activities Committee, and he accused Welch of having tried to get Fisher named, despite this, "as the assistant counsel for this committee."

"Now I have hesitated bringing that up," McCarthy said, adopting his pose as the fairest of men, "but I have been bored with your phony request to Mr. Cohn here that he personally get every Communist out of government before sundown. Therefore we will give you the information about the young man in your own organization.

"Now I'm not asking you at this time why you tried to force him on this committee. That you did, the committee knows. . . ."

It instantly became apparent that the committee knew nothing of the sort. Senator Mundt, who in the past had supported McCarthy, broke into McCarthy's tirade, saying:

"The Chair wishes to say that he has no recognition or no memory of Mr. Welch recommending Mr. Fisher or anybody else as counsel for this committee."

Welch was staring at McCarthy. He no longer resembled the puckish actor. His face had gone white with anger.

"Senator McCarthy," he began in a voice that shook, "I did not know, Senator—Senator, sometimes you say, 'May I have your attention.' May I have yours, Senator?"

McCarthy turned his back and walked over to James Juliana, calling loudly for a newspaper clipping about Fisher.

"I'm listening to someone in one ear and you in the other," he told Welch.

"Now this time, sir, I want you to listen with both," Welch snapped.

"Yes, sir."

McCarthy, boldly indifferent, went right on giving instructions to Juliana about material he wanted to place in the record.

"Senator, you won't need anything in the record when I finish telling you this," Welch said, his voice still shaking with emotion, tears glistening in his eyes. "Until this moment, Senator, I think I never really gauged your cruelty or your recklessness.

"Fred Fisher is a young man who went to Harvard Law School and came into my firm and is starting what looks to be a brilliant career with us. When I decided to work for this committee I asked Jim St. Clair, who sits on my right, to be my first assistant. I said to him, 'Jim, pick somebody in the firm to work under you that you would like.'

"He chose Fred Fisher and they came down on an afternoon plane. That night when we had taken a little stab at trying to see what the case was about, Fred Fisher and Jim St. Clair and I went to dinner together.

"I then said to these young men: 'Boys, I don't know anything about you except I've always liked you, but if there's anything funny in the life of either one of you that would hurt anybody in this case, you had better speak up quick.'

"And Fred Fisher said: 'Mr. Welch, when I was in law school and for a period of months after, I belonged to the Lawyers' Guild,' as you have suggested, Senator.

"He went on to say, 'I am the secretary of the Young Republicans' League with the son of the Massachusetts

Governor and I have the respect and admiration of the twenty-five lawyers or so in Hale and Dorr [Welch's law firm]."

"And I said, 'Fred, I just don't think I'm going to ask you to work on the case. If I do, one of these days that will come out and go over national television and it will hurt like the dickens.'

"So, Senator, I asked him to go back to Boston. Little did I dream you could be so reckless and so cruel as to do an injury to that lad. It is true he is still with Hale and Dorr. It is true he will continue to be with Hale and Dorr.

"It is, I regret to say, equally true that I fear he shall always bear a scar, needlessly inflicted by you. If it were in my power to forgive you for your reckless cruelty, I would do so. I like to think I'm a gentle man, but your forgiveness will have to come from someone other than me."

The Senate Caucus Room was hushed, its audience spellbound. Few there probably realized how thoroughly McCarthy had exposed himself. Far from trying to get the committee to hire Fisher, Welch had sent him back to Boston as he had said; and in trying to anticipate McCarthy's moves and lessen the damage he might do, he had disclosed the action and the reasons for it at the time. The *New York Times* had carried the story and had used Fisher's picture; but, despite all this, McCarthy had not been able to resist the savage lunge and the unprincipled accusation before a nationwide television audience.

Having made the gamble, even McCarthy could now feel the force of Welch's anger and contempt. He fumbled with some papers before him, and then he tried to bluster his way through the gathering storm, rumbling that Welch "has been baiting Mr. Cohn here for hours" and "I just want to give him this man's record. . . ."

Welch, the tears gone from his eyes, now had full control of himself. His eyes were cold and hard, his voice icy as he said: "Senator, may we not drop this? We know he belonged to the Lawyers' Guild."

"Let me finish this," cried McCarthy.

"And Mr. Cohn nods his head at me. I did you, I think, no personal injury, Mr. Cohn."

"No, sir."

"I meant to do you no personal injury, and if I did, I beg your pardon. Let us not assassinate this lad further, Senator. You've done enough. Have you no sense of decency, sir? At long last, have you left no sense of decency?"

"I know this hurts you, Mr. Welch," snarled McCarthy.

"I'll say it hurts."

"May I say, Mr. Chairman, as a point of personal privilege, that I'd like to finish this."

"Senator, I think it hurts you, too, sir," said Welch.

McCarthy rumbled on, trying to show that Welch had attempted to force Fisher upon the committee, a charge whose truth Mundt again denied. McCarthy then attempted to ask Welch a question, but Welch froze him with this final rejoinder:

"Mr. McCarthy, I will not discuss this further with you. You have sat within six feet of me and could ask, could have asked me about Fred Fisher. You have seen fit to bring it out, and if there is a God in Heaven it will do neither you nor your cause any good.

"I will not discuss it further. I will not ask Mr. Cohn any more questions. You, Mr. Chairman, may, if you will, call the next witness."

It was over. It took a few seconds for the realization to sink in; then the caucus room rocked with applause. Even press photographers, for the first time in the memory of Washington observers, were so moved they dropped their cameras and clapped for Welch. Senator Mundt, who had tried to prevent such demonstrations in the past, bowed his head as this one swept the hearing room, then quickly called a recess.

McCarthy sat slouched in his chair, breathing hard. Spectators and reporters shunned him. Feeling the universal hostility, he looked around, spread out his hands in puzzlement, and asked as if to himself:

"What did I do wrong?"

Joe McCarthy was destroyed in that one, dramatic scene. He had been exposed to millions as a low, unprincipled battler. He would never recover.

The Senate, so long cowed by him, was now prodded by Senator Flanders to censure him. Senators always hate to take action against one of their exclusive club, and it was perhaps a measure of McCarthy's offenses against decency that the Senate was finally impelled to investigate him.

There were more hearings, more wild flailing about by McCarthy. In typical McCarthy fashion, he denounced mild-mannered Senator Arthur V. Watkins, a Utah Republican and chairman of the investigating committee. Watkins, he charged, was "cowardly" and "stupid"; the Watkins committee was serving as the "unwitting handmaiden," the "involuntary agent," and "attorneys in fact" of the Communist Party.

It was too much to be borne. The Senate voted 67–22 to "condemn" McCarthy, not to "censure" him. His followers attempted to find some hope in that fact, but the effect was the same. McCarthy had been discredited and repudiated.

His collapse, both politically and physically, was incredibly swift. He wandered the halls of the Senate like some pale ghost of his former self. Where the press had hung on his every word in the glory days of the witch hunt, his speeches were now almost automatically consigned to the wastebasket. Always a heavy drinker, he drank more and more heavily—and carried it less well. Finally, on April 28, 1957, he was taken to the Bethesda Naval Hospital, where he had been treated several times previously, and there at 6:02 P.M. on May 2, he died. The cause of death was described as "peripheral neuritis," an affliction of the nervous system often associated with the disease of alcoholism.

Even in death, he was not forgotten, not without influence. There were still millions of Americans who believed that he really had been leading a great "crusade" against communism. A Gallup poll taken in August, 1954, after his damaging self-exposure at the Army-McCarthy hearings, showed that 51 per cent of all Americans opposed McCarthy, but—what was truly surprising—36 per cent, an enormous number, still had unshaken faith in him. They still believed—and much evidence indicates that many still do—that there were Communists everywhere and that all our troubles had been caused by conspiracy and betrayal.

Yet the facts were undeniable. Beginning in the Truman Administration, every government employee, no matter how low his position, was investigated by departmental security agencies and the FBI. If there was *anything* in his record to cause a doubt or a suspicion, the employee was automatically suspended. He could appeal, but he was always at a disadvantage. He was not permitted to face his accusers; he could not cross-examine them. He was not permitted even to know who they were. In a reversal of all American tradition, the government did not have to prove an employee's guilt; it did not really have to prove anything. He had to prove—and prove beyond a shadow of a doubt—his complete innocence and trustworthiness.

This evidence, taken at appeal hearings, was passed on by loyalty boards composed of conservative Democrats and Republicans. President Truman, in an effort to avoid just the kind of demagogic hue and cry McCarthy had raised, had placed conservative and life-long Republicans in charge of the State Department's Loyalty Board and the top Loyalty Review Board. Under these circumstances it is hardly enough to say the dice were loaded; they were double-loaded.

Yet out of nearly 5 million federal employees screened during the Truman Administration, only 560—about one-hundredth of 1 per cent—were dismissed "on grounds relating to loyalty." McCarthy and the Republicans, of course, clamored that the Truman system was too lax; they would tighten the net so that not even a gnat could get through. Yet the Eisenhower Administration found it practically impossible to justify this pet theory. On February 18, 1954, it reported there had been some 2,200 "security risk" firings, but only 29 involved disloyalty. This figure was so small it was ridiculous, and so repeated and transparent efforts were made to revise it upward. In the next month, the figures were changed again and again until the administration finally proclaimed in March, 1954, that out of 2,429 dismissals, 422 involved "subversives." Even if one discounts the constant shifting of the figures, even if one accepts this 422 tally as genuine, it didn't spell out the presence of a menace. There were then some 2.5 million federal employees; and even if 422 had finally rested under the shadow of a "doubt," this still represented less than two-hundredths of 1 per cent of all government workers.

Those were the facts, but a demagogue does not deal in facts. He deals in fear, in blind unreasoning emotion, in hate and prejudice. Joe McCarthy knew and practiced the art as has no other demagogue in American history. He turned the nonexistent into a menace. He trampled on justice and fair play. He disgraced his country at home and abroad—and made millions believe they were following him in a holy crusade. Such is the power of the supreme demagogue; such, the lesson of Joe McCarthy.

INDEX